NEW MEXICO CAR ACCIDENT CLAIMS

A 505 LEGAL GUIDE

KENNETH H. STALTER

Copyright © 2026 by Kenneth H. Stalter
All rights reserved.

Published by Stalter Law LLC, a subsidiary of 505 Legal, P.C.
PO Box 90336, Albuquerque, NM 87199
www.505legal.com

No part of this book may be reproduced, stored in a retrieval system, or transmitted in any form or by any means, electronic, mechanical, photocopying, recording, or otherwise, without the prior written permission of the publisher.

Library of Congress Cataloging-in-Publication Data
Stalter, Kenneth H.
New Mexico Car Accident Claims: A 505 Legal Guide / Kenneth H. Stalter
ISBN: 979-8-9928381-2-1

Printed in the United States of America
First Edition: 2026

Dedicated to the clients who trusted me with their cases. You taught me more than you know.

CONTENTS

About 505 Legal — vii
About 505 Legal Guides — ix
About the Author — xi
A Few Important Notes — xiii
Introduction — xv

Part 1: Getting the Right Help — 1

1. Who This Book Is For — 3
2. Why Most People Need a Lawyer — 10
3. Finding the Right Attorney — 18
4. Understanding Fee Agreements — 27
5. What to Expect from Your Lawyer (and What They Expect from You) — 35

Part 2: Understanding Your Case — 43

6. How Auto Insurance Actually Works — 45
7. Uninsured and Underinsured Motorist Claims — 53
8. Medical Treatment and Your Claim — 61
9. Getting Your Bills Paid While Your Case Is Pending — 68
10. Property Damage — 76
11. What Your Case Is Worth — 85

12	Negotiating a Settlement	95
13	When Your Case Goes to Court	107
14	Closing Your Case and Getting Paid	115

Part 3: Special Situations — 123

15	Medicare and Your Injury Claim	125
16	Claims Involving Children	131
17	Wrongful Death Cases	136
18	Insurance Bad Faith	142

Conclusion	149
Appendix A: Glossary of Terms	151
Appendix B: What To Do Immediately After an Accident	161
Appendix C: Questions to Ask Before Hiring a Lawyer	163
Appendix D: Questions to Ask Your Lawyer During Your Case	167
Appendix E: Document Checklist	171

ABOUT 505 LEGAL

505 Legal was co-founded by Farmington criminal defense attorney Shellie Patscheck and Albuquerque insurance attorney Kenneth Stalter because we saw a problem in New Mexico.

Communities across the state—especially outside the big metro areas—were losing attorneys. The traditional hometown lawyer, the person you could turn to when legal trouble found you, was disappearing. But we also recognized the limits of that traditional model: the solo generalist, pulled in too many directions, often lacked the depth that serious cases require.

We wanted to build something different. A modern hometown law firm that uses contemporary tools and systems to deliver focused expertise—while maintaining the accessibility and community roots that made hometown lawyers valuable. A top-notch, local legal team rather than a single overwhelmed attorney.

Too many people encounter the legal system on one of the worst days of their lives. They then find themselves overwhelmed by noise, pressure, and half-truths.

We believe informed clients make better decisions, even when those decisions are difficult. We believe people should be participants in their cases, not passengers. And we believe good legal work is measured not by slogans or verdict headlines, but by whether the outcome serves the client's goals.

ABOUT 505 LEGAL GUIDES

Publishing plain-English legal guides is part of our mission at 505 Legal.

We want the people we serve to understand the processes they're facing—not because understanding replaces professional help, but because it makes professional help work better. An informed client asks better questions, spots problems earlier, and makes decisions with confidence.

These guides cover legal topics that matter to everyday New Mexicans. Each one is written for people with no legal background, focused on practical steps rather than theory. The goal is always the same: to turn readers into active participants in their own cases.

We hope you'll choose 505 Legal when you need an attorney. But even if you don't, we hope these guides help you wherever you go.

ABOUT THE AUTHOR

Kenneth H. Stalter was born in Albuquerque and returned to New Mexico after graduating from Harvard Law School. He has worked on both sides of the courtroom—as a prosecutor handling felony trials, as general counsel for the New Mexico Attorney General's Office, and now as co-founder of 505 Legal.

His current practice focuses on civil litigation, with an emphasis on injury and insurance claims, civil rights, and government accountability. He also holds a master's degree in cybersecurity, which informs his approach to the increasingly data-driven systems that shape modern insurance practices.

He wrote this book because he believes injured people deserve to understand the process they're facing. The insurance system isn't designed to explain itself to you. This guide is.

A FEW IMPORTANT NOTES

This book provides general information about car accident claims in New Mexico. It is not legal advice for your specific situation.

Every case is different. Legal rules change. The same rule can apply differently depending on the facts involved. Nothing in this book can account for every scenario you might face.

Reading this book does not create an attorney-client relationship between you and the author or 505 Legal. It does not make Kenneth Stalter your lawyer.

This book is meant to help you work more effectively with an attorney, not to replace one. The legal system is complex, insurance companies are sophisticated, and the stakes in an injury claim are real. For most people, professional help is essential.

If you've been injured in a car accident in New Mexico, consult a qualified attorney about your specific circumstances. Use this book to prepare for that conversation, understand the process, and participate actively in your own case.

INTRODUCTION

If you're reading this, chances are you or someone you love has been in a car accident in New Mexico. You're facing a process you didn't ask for and probably don't understand. You want to know what happens next.

Maybe your car is totaled. Maybe you're still in pain weeks after the crash. Maybe you're missing work and wondering how you'll pay your bills while medical expenses pile up. The phone rings and it's someone from an insurance company asking questions. Papers arrive in the mail that you're not sure whether to sign.

It feels overwhelming. It feels like the system is bigger than you are.

Here's what most people don't realize until they're in the middle of it: the system isn't designed to help you.

That's not cynicism. It's just how the business works. Insurance companies are publicly traded corporations with shareholders expecting returns. Their adjusters are evaluated on how efficiently they close files—not on whether injured people feel whole at the end. The other driver's insurance company has no legal duty to you at all. Their obligation runs to their own customer, the person who hit you. Their job is to resolve your claim for as little as possible.

This creates a fundamental tension. You've been hurt through no fault of your own. You expect the responsible party's insurance to make things right. But the company across the table has every incentive to minimize what they pay you—and they have decades of experience doing exactly that.

Meanwhile, the injury law industry isn't always helping. Flip through late-night television or drive down the interstate and you'll see what passes for attorney advertising: promises of millions, aggressive slogans, faces on billboards. What those ads don't tell you is how those firms actually operate.

Some are case mills. They sign up as many clients as possible, then hand files off to paralegals and junior staff. You might never speak to the attorney whose face is on the billboard. Your case becomes a number in a system optimized for volume, not outcomes.

Some firms settle everything quickly—not because fast settlements serve their clients, but because quick turnover means more fees with less work. Insurance companies know which attorneys will take the first reasonable offer and which ones will actually prepare for trial. They adjust their behavior accordingly.

Others overpromise. They tell you your case is worth far more than any reasonable evaluation would support, then blame the insurance company or the jury when reality arrives. You spend months or years expecting a windfall that was never realistic.

None of this serves you. The insurance company wants to pay you less. Some attorneys want to process you faster. And you're caught in the middle, trying to recover from an injury while navigating a system that wasn't built with your interests in mind.

This book exists because you deserve better.

A Different Approach

At 505 Legal, we believe the attorney-client relationship should be a partnership, not a transaction.

That means we want informed clients—people who understand what's happening in their cases and why. We don't think knowledge is something to hoard. The more you understand, the better decisions you'll make, and the more effectively we can work together.

It also means we're honest about expectations. We're not going to tell you your case is worth a million dollars to get you to sign a retainer. We're going to tell you what we actually think, based on experience, even when that's not what you want to hear. Fairness is our goal—not maximizing a number at any cost.

Our approach to claims reflects this philosophy. We're methodical. Every step of the process—gathering records, identifying insurance coverage, building the demand package, negotiating or litigating—gets handled deliberately, not frantically. We communicate throughout, because you shouldn't have to wonder what's happening with your own case.

We think of ourselves as a modern hometown law firm. We use today's technology, systems, and insights to deliver the kind of focused expertise that a traditional small-town generalist couldn't provide—while maintaining the accessibility and community focus that made hometown lawyers valuable in the first place. You get a local legal team, not a single overwhelmed attorney juggling too many practice areas.

That's what 505 Legal is about. And that's why we publish guides like this one.

What This Book Will Do

This book walks you through the car accident claims process in New Mexico—from understanding how insurance actually works, to finding and working with an attorney, to navigating settlement negotiations or litigation.

By the end, you'll understand the landscape. You'll know what questions to ask. You'll be able to spot problems early and understand the decisions that arise along the way.

You'll be equipped to participate actively in your own case—not as a lawyer, but as an informed person who understands what's happening and why.

How to Use This Book

This is a reference, not a novel. Not every chapter will apply to your situation. Use the book however it's useful.

If you want a comprehensive view of what to expect from beginning to end, read straight through.

If you're just getting started and trying to figure out whether you need an attorney, start with Chapter 2. If you've already decided to hire someone and want to know what to look for, skip to Chapter 3.

If an insurance adjuster is pressing you to settle and you're not sure whether the offer is fair, Chapter 11 explains how cases are valued. Chapter 12 walks through how settlement negotiations actually work.

If you're feeling out of the loop with your attorney—or wondering whether the relationship is working—Chapter 5 covers what you should expect and how to raise concerns.

If the process feels like it's dragging on forever, Chapters 12 and 13 lay out realistic timelines. Knowing what's normal can make the waiting easier.

If your situation involves Medicare, a child's injuries, a death in the family, or an insurance company acting in bad faith, Part III addresses those special circumstances.

Skim through to get a feel for the process. Read the chapters that address your immediate questions. Skip what doesn't apply. Return to specific sections as your case progresses and new issues arise.

Even if you only read the Key Takeaways at the end of each chapter, you'll be in a better position than most people facing this process for the first time.

The goal isn't to turn you into a lawyer. It's to turn you into an informed participant.

One more thing: this book assumes you're already at the claims stage — dealing with insurance, medical bills, and decisions about legal help. If you're reading this immediately after an accident, see Appendix B for the five most important things to do right now.

PART 1

GETTING THE RIGHT HELP

For most people, working with an attorney is the right call after a car accident. But hiring a lawyer doesn't mean handing everything off and waiting for a check. The best outcomes come from an active partnership between you and your legal team.

This section helps you find the right attorney, understand how fee agreements work, and know what to expect from the working relationship. By the end, you'll have the tools to be an active participant in your own case—someone who asks good questions, understands what's happening, and works alongside their attorney to achieve a fair result.

CHAPTER 1

WHO THIS BOOK IS FOR

You've been in a car accident. Or someone you love has.

Now you're facing phone calls from insurance companies, medical bills arriving in the mail, and a process you don't fully understand. Maybe your car is totaled. Maybe you're still in pain. Maybe you're missing work and wondering how you'll pay your bills.

You Don't Have to Be a Passive Participant

Most people go through a car accident claim feeling like things are happening *to* them. The insurance company calls. The adjuster asks questions. Offers get made. Papers need signing. And through it all, you're not quite sure if things are going the way they should.

This book is for anyone who wants to change that dynamic. You want to understand what's happening. You want to know your options. You want to be confident that your claim is being handled appropriately—whether you're handling it yourself or working with an attorney.

You want to be in the driver's seat.

Who Should Read This Book

This book is for you if you've been injured in a car accident in New Mexico and want to understand the process ahead of you.

It's for you if a family member was hurt and you're trying to help them navigate the system.

It's for you if you're thinking about hiring a lawyer but want to understand what that relationship should look like.

It's for you if you've already hired a lawyer and want to be an informed, active participant in your own case.

The only thing you need to get value from this book is a simple thought: *I want to know more about this so I can make better decisions.*

That's it. You don't need a legal background. You don't need to have been through this before. You just need to be willing to learn.

People Come to This Process with Different Expectations

Some people feel completely at the mercy of the system. They assume the insurance company holds all the cards, and there's nothing they can do but accept whatever they're offered.

Others come in confident. They've been successful in business, in a profession, or in other areas of life. They figure they can handle this themselves and get a good result.

Still others have wildly unrealistic ideas about what their case might be worth—sometimes too high, sometimes too low. They've heard stories from friends, seen headlines in the news, or watched too many lawyer commercials.

All of these people can benefit from understanding how the process actually works.

Whether you feel powerless or overconfident, whether your expectations are too high or too low, this book will give you a clearer picture of the landscape. With that picture, you'll make better decisions.

What This Book Will Do

This book provides a general overview of how car accident injury claims work in New Mexico. By understanding these principles, you'll be better positioned to seek a fair resolution to your claim.

You'll learn how auto insurance actually works—including parts that might surprise you.

You'll understand what happens during the claims process, from the first phone call to the final settlement check.

You'll know what to look for when hiring an attorney, and what to expect once you've hired one.

You'll learn how to ask the right questions, spot potential problems, and understand the decisions that need to be made along the way.

Most importantly, you'll be equipped to participate actively in your own case. Not as a lawyer—but as an informed person who understands what's happening and why.

What This Book Will Not Do

Let me be clear about the limits of what any book can offer.

This book will not substitute for a lawyer. Reading it won't make you qualified to handle a complex injury claim on your own. It will help you understand the process, but understanding the process is not the same as navigating it.

This book will not cover every possible situation. Car accidents involve countless variables—different injuries, different insurance policies, different drivers, different circumstances. I'll cover the principles that apply broadly, but your situation will have details that no book can anticipate.

This book will not make decisions for you. Should you settle or go to trial? Is that offer fair? Those are judgment calls that depend on facts I don't know about your case.

This book will not make the process easy. Injury claims take time. They involve frustration, uncertainty, and patience. Understanding the process helps, but it doesn't eliminate the difficulty.

This book will not reveal any silver bullets, weird tricks, or secret loopholes. There aren't any. Anyone who tells you otherwise is selling something you probably shouldn't buy.

This book will not guarantee results. No one can.

This book will not tell you what your case is worth. That depends on your injuries, your medical treatment, the available insurance, and a dozen other factors specific to you.

What this book *will* do is help you understand the legal landscape so you can work effectively with your lawyer to pursue a fair outcome.

A Word About Artificial Intelligence

I'm tech-savvy. I use AI tools daily in my work. And I'm telling you: be extremely cautious about using AI to evaluate injury claims or legal principles.

AI is a powerful tool for research and brainstorming. It can help you develop questions. It can help you think through strategies. But it is not reliable for conclusions.

Here's the problem. I could prompt an AI to tell you your car crash is worth ten million dollars. I could prompt a different AI—or the same one with different instructions—to tell you your case is worth nothing and you're wasting your time. The output depends entirely on how the question is framed, what context is provided, and what the AI has been trained on.

AI doesn't understand the nuances of your situation. It doesn't know New Mexico law the way an experienced attorney does. It can sound confident while being completely wrong.

Use AI to help you think. Use it to generate questions. But don't use it to reach conclusions about your injury claim. That's what lawyers—and books like this one—are for.

Why New Mexico Matters

Most of the insurance companies you'll deal with are based out of state. Some are national carriers. Some are regional. For almost all of them, New Mexico is an afterthought.

That might not seem like a big deal, but it matters. New Mexico has unique rules about car insurance. Our laws around uninsured motorist coverage, for example, are different from other states. Insurance adjusters—even those licensed to work in New Mexico—aren't necessarily trained on these distinctions.

Any injury claim arising from a New Mexico accident has to account for these realities. This book is written specifically for that context. The principles here apply to New Mexico law, New Mexico courts, and the particular challenges and opportunities that come with pursuing a claim in our state.

You Can Do This

Here's what I want you to take away from this first chapter: this process is not as intimidating as it might seem.

You don't need to understand every technical detail of insurance law. You don't need to memorize statutes or learn legal jargon. You don't need to become a lawyer.

You just need to understand enough to participate. Enough to ask good questions. Enough to recognize when something doesn't seem right.

Key Takeaways

- This book is for anyone injured in a New Mexico car accident who wants to understand the process and participate actively in their claim.
- The only prerequisite is wanting to make better decisions.
- This book won't substitute for a lawyer, guarantee results, or tell you what your case is worth. It will help you understand the landscape.
- Be cautious with AI tools—they're useful for questions and research, but not for conclusions about your claim.

- New Mexico has unique insurance rules that out-of-state carriers may not fully understand. This book is written for that reality.
- You don't need to become a legal expert. You just need to understand enough to participate.

CHAPTER 2

WHY MOST PEOPLE NEED A LAWYER

You've been in a car accident. It wasn't your fault. The other driver ran a red light, or rear-ended you at a stoplight, or crossed the center line. The police came. A report was filed. The other driver's insurance company will pay for your damages. That's how it works, right?

Not exactly.

The Misconception

Most people believe insurance companies make things right after an accident. You can't blame them. Watch any insurance commercial and you'll see friendly agents, reassuring slogans, and lots of promises. The message is clear: when something goes wrong, we're here to help.

Here's what those commercials don't tell you. The other driver's insurance company has limited legal duty to you. Their duty runs to their client—the person who hit you. Their job is to protect their insured, typically by resolving your claim for as little money as possible.

Let that sink in. The company you're about to call for help has a financial incentive to pay you less.

The Early Offer Trap

A few days after the accident, the adjuster calls. They're polite. They express concern about your injuries. Then they make an offer. Maybe $2,500. Maybe $5,000.

If you've only been to urgent care, that number might look good. Your car is damaged, you're sore, you missed a day of work. A few thousand dollars would help right now.

But here's what you don't know yet. Six months from now, you might still be in physical therapy. You might be seeing a pain specialist. You might have medical bills that dwarf that early offer.

To get any money from the insurance company, you'll need to sign a release. That release is final. It covers everything—past, present, and future. Once you sign, you cannot go back for more. Ever.

The insurance company knows this. That's why they call early.

The Phone Call You Didn't Expect

Let's say you don't take the early offer. You call the adjuster to explain what happened, expecting a straightforward conversation. You're the victim here. You just need to tell your story and they'll process your claim.

Instead, the questions start.

What were you doing right before the accident? Were you reaching for something? Adjusting the radio? Looking at your phone? Did you have both hands on the wheel? What did you have for breakfast? Did you drink alcohol the night before? Were you on your way to work? What time did your shift start?

Suddenly you feel like a suspect. You came into this call as the victim. Now you're defending yourself.

This isn't an accident. The adjuster is doing their job.

Why All Those Questions Matter

New Mexico is a comparative negligence state. That means if you share any fault for the accident—even a little—your recovery gets reduced.

Here's an example. Say your case is worth $30,000. The other driver ran a red light, clearly at fault. But the insurance company argues you were glancing at a bag of chips on the passenger seat when the collision happened. A jury might find you 10% responsible.

Now your $30,000 case is worth $27,000.

That's why adjusters ask about your breakfast. About your phone. About every moment leading up to the crash. They're looking for anything that shifts fault onto you.

They're also looking for pre-existing conditions. Old injuries. Anything that suggests your current pain isn't really from this accident. And they're evaluating your credibility. Do you seem like someone a jury would believe?

Every answer you give is being used to build a case—against you.

When People Realize They Need Help

Some people figure this out after a few frustrating phone calls. The process isn't what they expected. They're not getting answers. They feel like they're fighting rather than being helped.

Others realize it when they see the release the insurance company wants them to sign. Legal language. Finality. The weight of what they're being asked to give up becomes real.

Some people realize it when they understand what they're actually up against. Insurance companies have spent decades building systems—algorithms, databases, automated processes—designed to resolve claims quickly and cheaply. The adjuster you're negotiating with may have limited authority to deviate from what those systems recommend. You're not just negotiating with a person. You're pushing against a machine.

More and more people are figuring it out before they even talk to the other driver's insurance company. They understand that professional help usually leads to better results.

There's no wrong time to call an attorney. But earlier is usually better than later—especially before you've signed anything or given a recorded statement.

One more reason timing matters: statutes of limitations. In New Mexico, most car accident injury claims must be filed within three years. That sounds like a long time — until months slip by while you're focused on recovery, and suddenly it isn't.

Three years is the general rule, but variations exist. Cases involving government employees have different deadlines. Claims against your own insurance company may have different rules. This is an area where you don't want to take chances.

What a Lawyer Actually Does

You might think hiring a lawyer just means having someone negotiate on your behalf. That's part of it. But an experienced personal injury attorney does much more, even before your case gets anywhere near a courtroom.

Managing deadlines. Your attorney should identify, calendar, and track important deadlines like the statute of limitations that applies to your claim.

Gathering your medical records and bills. This sounds simple. It isn't. Medical providers use different systems. Physicians bill separately from hospitals. Bills arrive months after treatment. An attorney's office has processes for tracking all of it down.

Handling subrogation. If your health insurance paid for accident-related treatment, they may have a right to be repaid from your settlement. This is called subrogation. Miss this step and you could face serious problems later—including demands for repayment after you've already spent the money. Medicare has its own complex rules that carry legal penalties for noncompliance.

Finding all available insurance. The at-fault driver's liability policy isn't always the only source of recovery. What if they don't have enough coverage? Your own uninsured or underinsured motorist policy might apply. Even policies on other cars in your household may come into play. An experienced attorney knows where to look.

Making sure your own insurance does its job. You may have medical payments coverage or UM/UIM coverage on your own policy. Your insurance company should open those claims and handle them properly. Sometimes they need prodding.

Gathering evidence. Crash reports. 911 recordings. Body camera footage from responding officers. Photographs from the scene. If the at-fault driver was cited or prosecuted, court records. An attorney knows how to obtain all of it.

Building a professional demand package. This is the document that presents your case to the insurance company. It pulls together the evidence, the medical records, the bills, and the legal arguments. It looks different from a handwritten letter.

Valuing your claim. What is your case actually worth? An attorney who handles these cases regularly knows how similar injuries have settled. They know what juries in New Mexico have awarded. They can calibrate a demand that reflects reality.

Evaluating punitive damages. Was the at-fault driver drunk? Texting? Fleeing from police? Certain conduct opens the door to punitive damages—a money judgment meant to punish, not just compensate. Identifying and substantiating this evidence requires legal knowledge.

The signaling effect. Insurance companies track attorneys. They know who files lawsuits. They know who goes to trial. They know who settles every case. When an attorney with a reputation for trying cases sends a demand letter, it changes how the insurance company evaluates the claim.

If your case goes to court, there's litigation on top of all this. Filings. Discovery. Depositions. Motions. Trial. That's a different level entirely.

When You Don't Need a Lawyer

Not every car accident requires an attorney. If your claim is small enough that attorney fees would eat up most of the recovery, it may not make economic sense.

Attorneys typically work on contingency in personal injury cases, meaning they take a percentage of what you recover. For small claims, that math doesn't work for either side.

If you only have property damage—your car got hit but you weren't injured—you can probably handle that yourself.

The Bottom Line

Here's what I tell people who aren't sure they need a lawyer: if you're not convinced I'm adding value, it's probably not a good fit. I'm not selling used cars. There's plenty of work out there. If you think you can do just as well on your own, go for it.

But I encourage you to read through this book first.

Think about whether you have the time to gather every medical record and bill. Think about whether you understand subrogation rules and Medicare compliance. Think about whether you can identify every insurance policy that might apply to your situation. Think about whether you're ready for the questions the adjuster will ask—and whether you know how your answers will be used.

Then decide.

Key Takeaways

- The at-fault driver's insurance company has limited legal duty to you. Their job is to protect their client by paying you as little as possible.
- Early settlement offers are designed to close your claim before you know what your injuries will cost.
- New Mexico's comparative negligence rule means any fault attributed to you reduces your recovery.
- Attorneys add value by finding additional coverage, gathering evidence, handling complex legal requirements, and signaling to insurance companies that you're serious.
- For small claims or property-damage-only situations, you may not need a lawyer.
- Before you decide to handle an injury claim without a lawyer, read this book and consider whether it really makes sense to do all on your own.

CHAPTER 3

FINDING THE RIGHT ATTORNEY

You've decided you need a lawyer. Now what?

Finding the right attorney matters. This could be a relationship that lasts years. The person you choose will handle a significant financial matter on your behalf. You need someone you trust, someone who communicates clearly, and someone who knows what they're doing.

Here's how to find that person.

Start with People You Trust

The best way to find an attorney is through someone who has actually worked with one. Not someone who saw a billboard. Not someone who heard a name somewhere. Someone who hired an attorney, went through a case, and can tell you what the experience was really like.

Ask around. A friend, family member, or coworker who has been through a car accident claim can tell you things no advertisement ever will. Did the attorney return calls? Did they explain things clearly? Did the client feel respected throughout the process? Did they get a result they felt good about?

If someone you trust had a good experience with an attorney, that's worth more than any marketing budget.

What Ads Can and Can't Tell You

Most people start their search with advertising. Google results, television commercials, billboards along the interstate. That's natural. You go with what's familiar.

There's nothing wrong with using ads as a starting point. But understand what they are: marketing. An ad tells you that an attorney or firm spent money to reach you. It doesn't tell you whether they'll do a good job on your case.

The only way to know if an attorney is right for you is to ask questions.

What Actually Separates Good from Mediocre

Three things matter most when evaluating a personal injury attorney.

Do they listen? Any good attorney begins with a genuine effort to understand your situation. Not just the facts of the accident, but your goals. What matters to you? What are you worried about? What outcome would make this feel resolved? An attorney who jumps to conclusions without listening isn't someone you want handling your case.

Do they do this routinely? A general practice attorney can handle a basic car accident claim. But it's often impossible to know at the beginning whether your case is basic or complex. An attorney who handles injury claims regularly will spot issues that a generalist might miss.

Can they handle insurance complexity? This is the real differentiator. Any accident can take a turn where insurance issues become critical. What if the at-fault driver's insurance company denies coverage? Is the denial valid? Can it be challenged? What if we need to pursue your own uninsured or underinsured motorist coverage? Was the coverage selection valid? Is there an argument for more coverage?

An attorney who only understands liability claims—who did what to whom—may not be equipped to navigate these questions. An attorney with deep experience in insurance issues can make a real difference when complications arise.

Why the Numbers Don't Mean Much

You'll see firms advertise case volume, average settlements, or headline verdicts. These numbers feel meaningful. They're not.

Think about it. As the number of cases a firm handles goes up, the average settlement almost has to go down. More cases means more smaller cases in the mix. A high volume of cases at lower values doesn't indicate skill. It might just reflect the population the firm serves.

What about million-dollar verdicts? Those happen when injuries are catastrophic and insurance coverage is substantial. An attorney who won a million-dollar verdict can't replicate that result on your case unless your injuries and coverage justify it. What somebody else got doesn't tell you what your case is worth.

Settlement values depend on factors the attorney doesn't control: how badly you were hurt, how much insurance is available, how clear the liability is. Judging an attorney by their settlement numbers is like judging a doctor by their patients' heights.

Get away from the numbers. Get back to the relationship.

Ask yourself: Has this person taken the time to explain things clearly? Do I feel like they understand my situation? Can I see myself working with them for potentially years?

Questions to Ask

When you meet with an attorney, come prepared. These questions will help you evaluate whether this person is the right fit.

- How will we know when it's time to settle?
- Are your fees different if we file a lawsuit? If we go to trial?
- Will I receive a cost breakdown before settling?
- How do you advise clients who aren't sure whether a settlement offer is appropriate?
- What will you do to investigate the insurance situation?
- What's your approach to litigating insurance coverage issues?
- Walk me through the claims negotiation process.
- Walk me through what litigation looks like.
- How will you investigate this case?

Pay attention to how the attorney answers, not just what they say. Are they patient? Are they clear? Do they treat you like a partner in this process, or like someone to be managed?

An attorney's willingness to explain things thoroughly tells you a lot about how they'll treat you throughout your case.

Red Flags

Some things should make you walk away.

High-pressure sales techniques. If an attorney tells you that you need to sign up right now, that's a red flag. A legitimate attorney doesn't need to pressure you into a decision.

Confusing fee arrangements. Fee structures should be clear and straightforward. Be especially wary of fees that escalate if certain things happen, like filing a lawsuit. That creates a perverse incentive for the attorney to avoid litigation even when it would benefit you.

Guarantees or promises of results. No attorney can guarantee an outcome. They don't control enough variables. Anyone who promises you a specific result is either lying or doesn't understand their own profession.

Minimizing legitimate questions. If you ask a reasonable question and the attorney brushes it off, that's a problem. Your questions matter. An attorney who doesn't respect them now won't respect them later.

Claims of special insider status. Be skeptical of attorneys who suggest they have special relationships with adjusters or judges. That's not how this works.

Sign-up bonuses. If an attorney offers you money just to sign with them, walk away. This is exploitative, unethical, and possibly illegal.

Unsolicited contact. If an attorney contacted you after your accident without you reaching out first, that's a serious red flag. Ethical attorneys don't chase ambulances.

Yellow Flags

Some things aren't necessarily problems, but they might mean this isn't the right fit.

Maybe the attorney seemed rushed or inattentive. Maybe their explanations didn't quite make sense to you. Maybe they lacked confidence or clarity. Maybe you just felt like you were on different wavelengths.

None of these are deal-breakers on their own. But this relationship could last years. Fit matters. If something feels off, trust that instinct and keep looking.

What a "Consultation" Actually Is

The legal industry uses the word "consultation" in a way that creates mismatched expectations.

For you, "consultation" might suggest you'll get actionable legal analysis of your situation, whether or not you hire the attorney. That's not what happens. It's more like asking a doctor whether you need surgery before they've looked at your x-rays. Without investigation, no responsible attorney can tell you what your case is worth or how it will turn out.

For the attorney, a consultation is an opportunity to learn about your case and decide whether it makes sense to take it. They'll ask questions about the accident, your injuries, and the insurance situation. They'll give you general information about the process. But they won't—and shouldn't—give you specific legal advice before they've done their homework.

In New Mexico, consultations for personal injury cases are typically free. This is especially true for cases that will be handled on contingency. Expect the initial meeting to last fifteen to thirty minutes. That's usually enough time for an attorney to determine whether they can help.

Should you meet with multiple attorneys? Here's a simple test. After that first meeting, ask yourself: Did I feel treated with respect? Will I be comfortable entrusting this person with a significant financial matter? Can I see myself working with them for potentially years?

If you can answer yes, sign with that attorney. If you have doubts, keep looking.

New Mexico's Legal Landscape

Here's a reality about New Mexico: most cities and towns are small. Many have few attorneys. Some have none.

That creates a challenge. The traditional solo practitioner in a small community is often a generalist — handling injury claims alongside divorces, criminal defense, wills, and real estate. They may be perfectly competent, but they may not have deep experience with the insurance complexities that can make or break an injury case.

The old trade-off used to be: local generalist or distant specialist. Pick one.

That's changing. Some firms, like 505 Legal, are dedicated to delivering accessibility without sacrificing expertise — using modern technology, responsive communication, and client-focused systems to serve communities across the state. A team-based approach, where attorneys concentrate on specific practice areas rather than spreading thin across everything, means you're not giving up depth to get service.

What matters isn't whether your attorney's office is down the street. What matters is whether you can reach them when you need to, whether they have real experience in New Mexico courtrooms, and whether they know New Mexico injury and insurance law — not just general principles, but the specific rules and practices that apply here.

Look for a firm that's accessible and responsive, with dedicated experience in New Mexico injury and insurance claims — not a solo generalist juggling too many practice areas, and not a distant billboard firm that treats you like a file number.

A Note on the Big Advertisers

You'll recognize some names from billboards and television. Some of those firms are excellent. Some are not. The advertising budget tells you nothing.

Ask questions. Is this a New Mexico firm, or an out-of-state operation looking at New Mexico as their next market? What's the firm's real presence in the state? Where are the attorneys from? Who will actually be working on your case? Is that person experienced in New Mexico courtrooms?

The name on the billboard might not be the person handling your file. Find out who will be.

Key Takeaways

- The best referral comes from someone who has actually worked with the attorney.
- Ads are a fine starting point, but they tell you nothing about quality. You have to ask questions.

- Look for attorneys who listen, handle injury cases routinely, and understand insurance complexity—not just liability.
- Ignore the numbers. Settlement values and case volume don't measure what matters.
- Red flags include high pressure, confusing fees, guarantees, insider claims, sign-up bonuses, and unsolicited contact.
- Consultations should be free, last about fifteen to thirty minutes, and are a mutual evaluation—not free legal advice.
- Look for a firm that's accessible and responsive, with real experience in New Mexico courtrooms and New Mexico injury and insurance law.
- For big advertising firms, find out who's actually doing the work and whether they have real New Mexico experience.

CHAPTER 4

UNDERSTANDING FEE AGREEMENTS

Before you sign anything, you need to understand how you're going to pay your attorney. Fee agreements in personal injury cases work differently than in other areas of law. The structure can work in your favor—but only if you understand what you're agreeing to.

This chapter explains how fees work, what to watch for, and how to avoid surprises when your case resolves.

How Contingency Fees Work

Most personal injury claims in New Mexico are handled on a contingency fee basis. This means the attorney's fee is calculated as a percentage of your total recovery. If you don't recover anything, you don't pay a fee.

That's the basis for all those ads you've seen: "No fee unless we win."

In New Mexico, contingency fees for injury claims typically range from one-third (33⅓%) to 40% of the total recovery. That percentage typically applies to the gross amount received from the insurance company—before deduction of costs, before payment of outstanding medical bills or subrogation claims, before anything else comes out.

One additional detail: attorneys in New Mexico must pay gross receipts tax on their fees, and this is usually added to the amount you pay. GRT rates vary across the state depending on what state and local governments have imposed in different cities and counties. The rate that applies to your case is typically based on where your attorney's office is located. Expect somewhere between 5% and 9% of the fee amount to be added for GRT.

So if your fee is 40% and the GRT rate is 8%, the total for attorney compensation would be 40% plus 3.2% (which is 8% of 40%), for a combined 43.2% of the recovery.

The Difference Between Fees and Costs

People often confuse fees and costs. They're different, and understanding the distinction matters.

Fees are what the attorney is paid for their time and expertise. Think of it like labor in auto repair or construction. Under a contingency agreement, if there's no recovery, the attorney fee is zero.

Costs are payments made to others to move your case forward. These include copying charges for medical records, filing fees in the court system, payments to court reporters who transcribe depositions, and fees for expert witnesses. Expert witness fees are often the largest cost component in cases that require them. Think of costs like parts or materials in the construction analogy.

Unlike construction, where materials might be the bigger expense, legal cases typically involve much higher labor (fees) than materials (costs). But costs can still add up, especially in complex cases or cases that go to trial.

In most contingency fee agreements, the attorney or firm will advance costs as they arise and then get reimbursed from the recovery at the end of the case. Fees are usually calculated before reimbursement of these costs.

One important note: some clients assume that if there's no recovery, the attorney will absorb the costs. This is generally not permitted under the rules of professional conduct. Paying a client's costs is considered prohibited financial assistance in connection with a pending matter. In most fee agreements, you remain obligated for costs even if the case doesn't result in a recovery. Make sure you understand this before you sign.

Why Fee Percentages Vary

You might wonder why one attorney charges 33⅓% while another charges 40%. Is the more expensive attorney better? Is the cheaper one cutting corners?

Usually, neither. The difference in fee percentages typically has nothing to do with the complexity of your case or the quality of the attorney. It's simply about how that attorney or firm has chosen to position themselves in the market. Most firms have a standard fee structure they apply to all contingency matters they handle.

A higher fee doesn't necessarily mean better representation. A lower fee doesn't necessarily mean worse. Focus on the attorney's qualifications, communication style, and experience—not on saving a few percentage points.

Escalating Fee Structures

Some fee agreements start at one percentage and increase if certain things happen. For example, the fee might be one-third before litigation but increase to 40% if a lawsuit is filed. Other triggers might include going to trial or filing an appeal.

Some reputable and ethical attorneys use this structure. The justification is that certain stages of a case—filing suit, going to trial—require significantly more of the attorney's time. That's fair as far as it goes.

But I'm not a fan of escalating fees. The problem is that strategic decisions on your claim can become influenced by the attorney's fee rates. If filing a lawsuit bumps the fee from 33% to 40%, is the attorney's recommendation to file suit driven by what's best for your case or by what's best for their bottom line?

This doesn't mean every attorney with an escalating fee structure is acting in bad faith. But it's a potential conflict you should be aware of. If you're considering an attorney with this structure, ask them directly how they handle the potential conflict. Their answer will tell you something.

Red Flags in Fee Arrangements

Most injury claims should be handled on contingency. If an attorney wants a deposit upfront or wants to charge you an hourly rate for a car accident injury case, be skeptical. The attorney may believe you don't have a viable case and just wants to bill you for their time regardless of the outcome.

On the other end of the spectrum, if an attorney offers you money or some other financial assistance to sign up with them, that's a serious red flag. This is prohibited by the rules of professional conduct. Walk away.

What to Look for Before You Sign

Before signing a fee agreement, make sure you understand these key points.

What happens if you fire the attorney? Even on contingency matters, if you discharge the attorney before the case resolves, you could owe them something—often calculated based on their time at an hourly rate. This is fair. Under a contingency arrangement, attorneys only get paid if there's a successful outcome. If you fire them before they have the chance to land the plane, they're entitled to compensation for the work they've done.

Who pays costs, and when? Know whether the attorney will advance case costs or whether they have the right to require trust deposits from you. It's reasonable for an agreement to include a provision allowing the attorney to stop advancing costs and require you to pay them directly. The attorney is not a bank. They shouldn't be required to bankroll a client's decision to run up costs when the prospects of recovery don't justify it—say, if you insist on going to trial despite receiving a fair settlement offer.

When can the attorney withdraw? Understand the circumstances under which the attorney can withdraw from your case and what happens to fees and costs if they do.

All of these provisions are permitted under the rules of professional conduct and are ethical. But you need to be aware of them before you sign, not after.

Common Surprises at Settlement Time

When your case settles and the check arrives, you might be surprised by what comes out of it.

Medical liens and subrogation. If your health insurance paid for accident-related treatment, they may have a right to be repaid from your settlement. If Medicare or Medicaid was involved, there are other rules. We'll cover this in detail later in the book, but know that your recovery may be reduced by these obligations.

Case costs. If your case required depositions, expert witnesses, or extensive record gathering, the costs can add up. This shouldn't be a complete surprise—there should be discussion along the way about what's happening and how much it costs. But clients sometimes underestimate how much these expenses total.

If You Already Have a Settlement Offer

Sometimes people come to an attorney after they've already received a settlement offer from the insurance company. If that's your situation, clarify one thing upfront: will the fee be calculated on the total settlement at the end, or just on the increase the attorney achieves for you?

Which approach is appropriate depends on the size of the offer you already have. If you come in with a typical lowball, pre-litigation offer—say, $3,000—an attorney would reasonably expect to calculate their fee on the total recovery. But if you come in with a substantial offer already on the table, the calculation might be different.

The key principle: you should not end up worse off for having hired counsel. A good attorney will structure the fee to make sure that's the case. Ask about this directly before signing.

Will the Other Side Pay My Attorney's Fees?

Clients sometimes ask whether the insurance company will be required to pay their attorney's fees on top of the settlement—as an add-on rather than something that comes out of their recovery.

In almost all cases, the answer is no. The insurance company will offer a single sum to resolve the case. They may factor potential attorney involvement into that number, but it's not broken out separately. The fee comes from your recovery.

In some cases, where there's an additional legal claim beyond typical negligence—certain statutory claims, for example—there may be grounds to seek an award of attorney's fees from the other side. If this possibility exists in your case, the fee agreement should address how that figures into the fee calculation.

Key Takeaways

- Most injury claims are handled on contingency: the attorney takes a percentage (typically 33⅓% to 40% in New Mexico) only if you recover money.
- Gross receipts tax (5–9%, depending on location) is added to the fee.
- Fees are for the attorney's work. Costs are payments to others—records, filing fees, experts. You typically remain obligated for costs even if there's no recovery.
- Fee percentages reflect the firm's market positioning, not case complexity.
- Escalating fees (rates that increase if you file suit or go to trial) create potential conflicts. Ask how the attorney handles this.

- Red flags: attorneys wanting deposits or hourly rates for injury cases, or offering money to sign up.
- Before signing, understand what happens if you fire the attorney, who pays costs, and when the attorney can withdraw.
- If you already have an offer, clarify how the fee will be calculated. You shouldn't end up worse off for hiring counsel.
- The other side typically won't pay your attorney's fees separately—the fee comes from your recovery.

CHAPTER 5

WHAT TO EXPECT FROM YOUR LAWYER (AND WHAT THEY EXPECT FROM YOU)

You've hired an attorney. Now what?

A personal injury case is a working relationship. It might last months. It might last years. Both sides have responsibilities. When expectations are clear from the start, everything goes smoother. When they're not, frustration builds on both sides.

This chapter explains what you should expect from your attorney, what your attorney expects from you, and how to keep the relationship on track.

The First Few Weeks

After you sign a fee agreement, the attorney's office gets to work gathering information. This phase is about building the file with everything needed to move your case forward.

On the crash itself, the firm needs whatever evidence you have—photos, the police report, witness information. They'll also gather what they can from law enforcement: the official crash report, 911 recordings, body camera footage if available.

On the medical side, they need to understand your current treatment status. What providers have you seen? What clinics? Are you still treating or are you finished? They'll also need your health insurance information, including whether you have Medicare or Medicaid. This matters for coordinating subrogation, liens, and compliance with rules around Medicare conditional payments.

On insurance, they need information about the at-fault driver's coverage and your own coverage. If a claim has already been opened, they'll need the claim number.

Your attorney must also identify critical deadlines — most importantly, the statute of limitations. Miss it and your claim is gone, no matter how strong the case. You shouldn't have to worry about this yourself, but you should confirm your attorney has it calendared and is working with that deadline in mind.

The first few weeks are all about populating the file with this basic information. From there, what happens next depends on where you are in your treatment.

If you're still treating, the case is likely in a holding pattern. The attorney can't make a demand until they know the full extent of your treatment. If you appear to be done treating, the firm may move toward preparing a demand or even filing litigation.

How Often Will You Hear from Your Attorney?

Communication depends on the stage of your case.

During treatment, don't expect frequent contact. If you're still seeing doctors and going to physical therapy, your attorney likely can't push the claim forward yet. You might hear from the firm every ninety days or so, just to check in and confirm your status. At this stage, communication is more about you keeping the attorney updated as your treatment progresses.

During litigation, communication should be more frequent. Unfortunately, many attorneys don't update clients as often as they should. Some only reach out when something notable happens. Look for a firm that has systems in place for routine updates so you're not left wondering what's going on with your own case.

One practical note: law firms are busy places. You should expect that some—or even most—of your conversations will be with staff members like paralegals or case managers rather than with the attorney directly. That's normal and doesn't mean your case isn't being handled properly.

But for any decision that needs to be made, the attorney should be involved. When it's time to evaluate a settlement offer, decide whether to file suit, or make any significant strategic choice, the attorney should be guiding you through it with adequate time and adequate explanation. If that's not happening, there's a problem.

What Your Attorney Expects from You

Your attorney needs you to do a few basic things.

Keep the firm updated on changes. If you move, change your phone number, get new health insurance, switch doctors, or start seeing a new provider, let your attorney's office know. Changes in your situation affect your case.

Respond when they contact you. If the firm reaches out and asks for something, it's because they need it to move your case forward. A request for a document, a signature, or a piece of information isn't busywork. Respond promptly.

Answer questions honestly and completely. Your attorney can only help you if they have accurate information. Don't leave things out because you think they might be embarrassing or unhelpful. Let your attorney decide what matters.

This isn't complicated. Stay in touch, respond to requests, and be honest. That's what makes someone a good client to work with.

The One Thing That Can Sink Your Case

Here's the most important thing I can tell you about your responsibilities as a client: don't lie.

Don't lie to your attorney. Don't lie to the insurance adjuster. Don't lie to the police. Don't lie in a deposition. Don't lie anywhere.

I can work with almost anything except a lie. If you made a mistake, tell me. If something embarrassing happened, tell me. If there's a fact that seems bad for your case, tell me. I need to know so I can deal with it. Surprises from the other side are far worse than uncomfortable truths shared early.

What about social media? I'd prefer you don't talk about your case or post about it online. But as long as what you're posting is truthful, it's not an insurmountable problem. The real issue isn't social media—it's honesty.

If you tell the insurance company your injuries keep you bedridden, and then you post a video of yourself dancing at a wedding, you have a problem. But that's a lying problem, not a social media problem. The platform just made the lie visible.

Tell the truth. Always.

At certain times, your attorney might advise you not to volunteer information, but whenever you do speak on a topic, it needs to be the truth.

When Relationships Break Down

Attorney-client relationships fail for predictable reasons.

Lack of communication. Either the attorney isn't keeping the client informed, or the client isn't responding to the attorney's requests. Both cause problems.

Misaligned expectations. The client expected the case to move faster, or settle for more than reality allows.

Lack of action by the attorney. The case sits without progress. Deadlines get missed. Nothing seems to be happening.

Clients withholding or misrepresenting information. The attorney discovers facts that should have been disclosed earlier. Trust breaks down.

Not understanding timelines. Injury cases take time. Clients who expect quick resolutions get frustrated when the process stretches on.

Most of these problems can be prevented with clear communication from the start. That's why this chapter exists.

If You're Unhappy with Your Attorney

If you feel like your attorney isn't doing their job, the first step is simple: contact them and explain your concerns.

There may be good reasons for what looks like inaction. Your attorney might be working hard behind the scenes, waiting on something outside their control, or failing to communicate progress adequately. A conversation might resolve everything.

If you reach out and don't get a response, that's a different situation. If you get a response but the explanation doesn't make sense, that's also a problem.

You have the right to know what's happening with your case. If your attorney can't or won't explain, you may need to consider whether this is the right fit.

A word of caution before you make that decision: review your fee agreement. Depending on the contract you signed, you may owe your current attorney for time spent, costs advanced, or a portion of any eventual recovery — even if you switch to someone else. Discharging your attorney is your right, but it's not always free. Understand the financial implications before you act.

A Word on Case Value Expectations

Some clients come in with unrealistic ideas about what their case is worth. Maybe a friend got a big settlement. Maybe they saw a headline about a massive verdict. Maybe they just assume injuries mean a large payout.

If you think your attorney is undervaluing your case, ask questions. Ask for examples of similar cases. Ask about prior settlements for comparable injuries. Then evaluate what you hear reasonably.

Although every case is different, your case is probably not as unique as you think. Attorneys who handle injury claims regularly have seen situations like yours before. Their valuation isn't arbitrary.

Here are some realities worth keeping in mind.

Big verdicts mean something horrible happened to someone. A million-dollar settlement usually means catastrophic, life-altering injuries. It's not something to hope for.

You haven't won the lottery. A settlement compensates you for real losses—medical bills, lost wages, pain and suffering. It's not a windfall.

If you can still work after your injury, you're going to need to keep working after your settlement. The money is meant to make you whole, not to fund early retirement.

The cases you see on the news made the news for a reason. They're rare. They're noteworthy. And they're often misunderstood or misrepresented in the coverage.

Talk to your attorney about valuation. Ask questions. But approach the conversation with realistic expectations.

Key Takeaways

- The first few weeks are about gathering information: crash evidence, medical records, insurance details.
- Communication frequency depends on the stage. During treatment, expect occasional check-ins. During litigation, expect more—but ask about the firm's update practices.
- You'll often talk to staff, not the attorney. But for decisions, the attorney should be involved with adequate time and explanation.
- Keep your attorney updated on changes. Respond to requests promptly.
- Don't lie. To anyone. Ever. This is the single most important thing you can do as a client.
- If you're unhappy, contact your attorney and explain your concerns. There may be good reasons—or there may be a real problem.
- Be realistic about case value. Big verdicts mean something terrible happened.

PART 2

UNDERSTANDING YOUR CASE

Insurance is complicated. Courts and the legal system are complicated. Resolving an injury claim means navigating both—and that creates some issues and pitfalls that can arise along the way.

This section walks you through how auto insurance actually works, what determines the value of your case, how settlement negotiations unfold, and what happens if your case goes to court. The goal isn't to make you an expert. It's to give you a point of reference so that when your attorney raises an issue or explains a development, you understand what's going on and why it matters.

CHAPTER 6

HOW AUTO INSURANCE ACTUALLY WORKS

You can't navigate a car accident claim if you don't understand how auto insurance works. Most people have a vague sense that insurance pays for things after an accident. But the details matter—and the details are where confusion lives.

This chapter explains the basic types of coverage, what the numbers on your policy actually mean, and how insurance companies really operate. Understanding this will help you make sense of everything that comes later.

The Main Types of Coverage

Auto insurance isn't one thing. It's a collection of different coverages, each with its own purpose. Here are the ones that matter most in a New Mexico car accident claim.

Liability coverage. This pays for bodily injury and property damage that the policyholder causes to others. New Mexico law requires all vehicles registered for public roads to carry liability coverage. Not all drivers comply, but that's the law.

If you're injured by another driver, their liability coverage is what you're dealing with. You're making a claim against their policy, not yours. Their insurance is supposed to compensate you for your injuries and repair or replace your vehicle.

Collision and comprehensive coverage. This is coverage on your own policy that pays for repairs to your vehicle, regardless of who was at fault. If you have collision coverage and your car is damaged in an accident, your insurance will pay to fix it—even if you caused the crash.

Medical payments coverage. This is coverage on your own policy that pays for medical bills after an accident, regardless of fault. Limits are usually modest—often no more than $5,000. But it can help cover immediate medical expenses while you sort out who was responsible.

Uninsured, underinsured, or unknown motorist coverage (UM/UIM). This is coverage on your own policy that protects you when someone else was at fault but they either don't have liability insurance, don't have enough liability insurance, or were never identified—like a hit-and-run driver.

UM/UIM coverage is important. We'll cover it in depth in the next chapter, but here's something many people don't realize: you can access this coverage even if you weren't in a vehicle when you were injured. If you were a pedestrian hit by a driver, your own auto policy's UM/UIM coverage can still apply.

Understanding Policy Limits

Insurance policies have limits—maximum amounts the policy will pay. Understanding how these limits work is essential.

Most bodily injury coverages are expressed as two numbers. You'll see something like $25,000/$50,000 or $100,000/$300,000. These represent the "per person" limit and the "per accident" limit.

The per person limit is the maximum amount any one injured person can receive from that policy. If the limit is $25,000 per person, that's the most you can get—no matter how serious your injuries.

The per accident limit is the maximum amount that everyone injured in the accident can collectively receive. This matters when multiple people are hurt.

Here's an example. Say four people are injured by an at-fault driver who has a policy with $25,000/$50,000 limits. Each injured person could theoretically receive up to $25,000. But all four of them together can only receive $50,000 total. That $50,000 gets divided among them, usually based on the seriousness of their injuries. Some or all of them will get less than the $25,000 per-person limit.

New Mexico's minimum required liability limits are $25,000 per person and $50,000 per accident for bodily injury. Many drivers carry only the minimum.

Why Minimum Limits Often Aren't Enough

Twenty-five thousand dollars sounds like a lot of money until you need medical care. Remember that New Mexico's minimum liability limits were set more than forty years ago—and haven't been updated since then. Meanwhile, the cost of medical care has grown astronomically.

Consider this scenario. You suffer a serious back injury in a crash and need surgery—a spinal fusion. This happens more often than you might think. That surgery alone could cost $150,000 or more. Add in recovery time, physical therapy, follow-up appointments, and lost wages, and the total damages climb higher.

Now imagine the at-fault driver has a policy with minimum limits: $25,000 per person.

That's all you're getting from their policy. Twenty-five thousand dollars. For $150,000 or more in medical bills, plus everything else.

What are your options? You could look for other policies the at-fault driver might have—an umbrella policy, for example. But few people carry umbrella coverage, and people with minimum limits policies are the least likely to have umbrella coverage.

You could try to recover from the driver's personal assets. But good luck collecting, even if they have any assets to pursue.

Or you could look to your own underinsured motorist coverage—if you have it, and if your limits are high enough.

This is why the coverage on your own policy matters, even when someone else caused the accident.

The "Full Coverage" Myth

People often say they want "full coverage" on their auto insurance. Insurance agents use the term too. Here's the problem: "full coverage" doesn't mean anything.

It's not a legal term. There's no agreed-upon definition. Different insurance companies and different sales agents use it to mean different things. One agent might mean liability plus collision plus comprehensive. Another might include medical payments. Another might assume UM/UIM coverage is part of it.

When people tell me they have "full coverage," I ask them what coverages they have and what their limits are. Often, they don't know.

Don't assume you have what you think you have. Pull out your policy. Look at the declarations page. See what coverages you're paying for and what limits apply to each one. If you don't understand what you're looking at, call your agent and ask them to explain it.

Why UM/UIM Coverage Matters

Uninsured and underinsured motorist coverage is optional in New Mexico. That means you can decline it. Many people do, because declining it saves money on premiums.

In my opinion, that's often a mistake.

If you're injured by a hit-and-run driver who's never identified, UM/UIM coverage is your only recourse. Without it, you have no one to make a claim against.

If you're injured by a driver who has insurance but only carries minimum limits, and your injuries are serious, $25,000 won't come close to covering your losses. Underinsured motorist coverage fills the gap—if you have it.

I understand the temptation to save money on insurance. But UM/UIM coverage can protect you when someone else fails to carry adequate insurance. In a state where the minimum limits are $25,000 and not everyone even carries that, it's worth having.

What Adjusters Actually Do

When you're injured in an accident, you'll deal with insurance adjusters. It helps to understand what their job actually is.

An adjuster's job is to process claims. But "process" doesn't mean "pay whatever is fair." It means resolve claims at minimum cost to the company, consistent with the company's duties to its policyholder.

Notice what's not in that description: doing what's best for you, the injured claimant.

The at-fault driver's insurance company has duties to the at-fault driver—their policyholder. Technically, the company has some duties to you as well but they are limited and difficult to enforce. The insurance company's goal is to close your claim for as little money as possible.

When an adjuster evaluates your claim, they're asking questions like: If we offer this amount, will they take it? If they turn it down and take us to court, what's our exposure? What will it cost to defend the case? What are similar cases settling for? How do we minimize the cost to the company while still protecting the insured from personal liability?

Nowhere in that analysis is the question: what's right for this injured person?

This isn't because adjusters are bad people. It's because that's not their job. Understanding this helps you approach the claims process with realistic expectations.

When There's No Insurance

What happens if the at-fault driver has no insurance at all?

Your recourse is your own policy. Medical payments coverage can help with immediate bills. UM coverage—the uninsured motorist portion—can provide compensation for your injuries. But you need to have these coverages in place before the accident happens.

What if you also don't have auto insurance at all?

Then your options are limited. Your health insurance, if you have it, will still cover medical treatment. But there's likely no recovery for pain and suffering, lost wages, or other damages. There's simply no policy to make a claim against.

This is another reason to maintain adequate coverage on your own vehicle, even if you're a safe driver. You can't control what other people do on the road.

Policy Exclusions You Might Not Expect

Insurance policies contain exclusions—situations where coverage doesn't apply. Some of these exclusions might surprise you.

For example, standard policies may exclude coverage if the driver was using the vehicle for rideshare services like Uber or Doordash. Were you driving for a delivery app when the accident happened? Your personal auto policy might deny the claim.

Here's something important: some exclusions that appear in policies aren't actually valid under New Mexico law. Insurance companies write policies for multiple states at once. An exclusion that's enforceable in Texas might not be enforceable in New Mexico. But the exclusion still appears in the policy, and the insurance company might still try to apply it.

If you're facing a coverage denial based on an exclusion, you need an attorney experienced in New Mexico coverage disputes. The exclusion might be legitimate, or it might not hold up under our state's law.

Key Takeaways

- Liability coverage is the at-fault driver's insurance that compensates you. Collision, medical payments, and UM/UIM are coverages on your own policy.
- Policy limits come in two numbers: per person and per accident. The per-accident limit gets divided among all injured parties.
- New Mexico's minimum liability limits ($25,000/$50,000) are often not enough for serious injuries.
- "Full coverage" isn't a real term. Know what coverages you have and what your limits are.
- UM/UIM coverage protects you when the at-fault driver has no insurance or not enough. Dropping it to save money is often a mistake.
- Adjusters work for the insurance company, not for you. Their job is to resolve claims at minimum cost.
- If the at-fault driver is uninsured and you have no auto insurance, your options for recovery are very limited.
- Some policy exclusions aren't valid under New Mexico law. If you're denied coverage, consult an attorney who knows NM insurance law.

CHAPTER 7

UNINSURED AND UNDERINSURED MOTORIST CLAIMS

If there's one type of coverage that people misunderstand, it's uninsured and underinsured motorist coverage. Most people don't know what it does. Many don't know they have it. Some declined it to save a few dollars on their premium without understanding what they were giving up.

This chapter explains what UM/UIM coverage is, when it applies, and why New Mexico's rules make it especially important to understand.

The Difference Between UM and UIM

Uninsured motorist coverage and underinsured motorist coverage sound similar, but they apply in different situations.

Uninsured motorist (UM) coverage applies when the at-fault driver has no liability coverage at all. This happens in a few ways. Maybe they never had a policy. Maybe their policy expired. Maybe their insurance company denied coverage because of an exclusion or a lapse in payment. Or maybe the at-fault driver was never identified—a hit-and-run where you never find out who hit you.

The common thread: the available liability coverage from the at-fault driver is zero. That's when UM coverage kicks in.

Underinsured motorist (UIM) coverage applies when the at-fault driver has some liability coverage, but it's not enough. UIM applies when two things are true: your damages exceed the at-fault driver's liability limits, and your UIM limits are higher than their liability limits.

If you're seriously injured and the at-fault driver only has a $25,000 policy, that $25,000 won't come close to covering your losses. UIM coverage helps fill the gap.

How UIM Offsets Work

Here's where it gets technical—and where people often get confused.

When you make a UIM claim, the insurance company typically gets to "offset" the at-fault driver's liability limits against your UIM limits. They subtract what was available from the other driver's policy.

Example: the at-fault driver has $25,000 in liability coverage. You have $50,000 in UIM coverage. You might think you have access to $75,000 total—$25,000 from their policy plus $50,000 from yours.

That's not how it works. With the offset, your UIM carrier subtracts the $25,000 liability coverage from your $50,000 UIM limit. You get $25,000 from the at-fault driver's liability policy, plus $25,000 from your UIM coverage ($50,000 minus the $25,000 offset). Total: $50,000, not $75,000.

I should note: there are ongoing legal disputes about exactly how these offset rules apply, depending on when your accident occurred and specific language in your policy. The law in this area continues to develop. If you're facing a UIM claim, consult a New Mexico insurance attorney to understand how the current rules apply to your situation.

New Mexico's Unique Rules

New Mexico has some of the most protective UM/UIM laws in the country. This matters because it means you may have access to more coverage than you think.

How UM/UIM must be sold. New Mexico has specific technical requirements for how insurance companies must offer UM/UIM coverage, how they can reduce UM/UIM limits below the policy's liability limits, and whether a complete rejection of UM/UIM coverage is valid. If the insurance company didn't follow these requirements, you may have more coverage than what's listed on your declarations page.

This isn't theoretical. These issues come up regularly, and policyholders often win when they challenge improperly reduced or rejected coverage.

Very few exclusions are valid. Under New Mexico law, most exclusions that insurance companies try to apply to UM/UIM coverage are not enforceable. Just because your carrier denied coverage based on an exclusion doesn't mean the denial will hold up. The exclusion might be invalid under our state's law.

If you've been denied UM/UIM coverage, that's not necessarily the end of the discussion. An attorney experienced in New Mexico coverage disputes can evaluate whether the denial is legally sound.

You don't have to be in the insured vehicle. This surprises many people. You can access UM/UIM benefits from your own policy even if you weren't in the car listed on that policy—even if you weren't in any car at all.

If you're a passenger in someone else's vehicle and get injured by an at-fault driver, you may be able to claim UM/UIM benefits from a policy you own, on a car that had nothing to do with the accident.

If you were riding a city bus and got injured, your own auto policy's UM/UIM coverage might apply.

If you were a pedestrian and got hit by a driver, same thing.

There are even cases in New Mexico where UM/UIM coverage applied to help victims of drive-by shootings—because the injury involved someone using a vehicle.

The coverage follows you, not just your car.

Stacking. New Mexico allows UM/UIM coverage to "stack" in certain circumstances. This means if you have multiple vehicles on your policy, or multiple policies in your household, your total available UM/UIM coverage may be higher than what any single policy shows.

Example: you have three cars, each with $25,000/$50,000 in UM/UIM coverage. With stacking, your actual total UM/UIM coverage could be $75,000/$150,000—three times the per-vehicle amount.

Whether stacking applies depends on how the policy is written and whether any reductions in coverage are valid under New Mexico law. Insurance companies often deny stacking or claim a particular policy doesn't apply. But those denials can be challenged in court, and these challenges succeed with some frequency.

The law here is technical and different from other states. Just because the insurance company says there's no stacking doesn't make it true. You need to talk to a New Mexico auto insurance attorney.

What UM/UIM Actually Covers

UM/UIM coverage pays for anything you could have recovered from the at-fault driver's liability coverage if it had been available.

That includes medical expenses, pain and suffering, lost income, and other out-of-pocket expenses related to your bodily injuries. Many out-of-state adjusters don't seem to understand this—they sometimes try to limit UM/UIM to just medical bills. That's wrong. UM/UIM covers the full range of compensatory damages.

In appropriate cases, punitive damages may also be recoverable under UM/UIM. If the at-fault driver's conduct was reckless or egregious, punitive damages might be part of the claim—and your UM/UIM carrier should account for that in evaluating your case.

UM/UIM also has a property damage component, often called UMPD. This covers damage to your vehicle and other property. If an uninsured driver crashes into your house, that's property damage to which UM/UIM could apply.

The Claims Process

When you make a UM/UIM claim, you're making a claim against your own insurance company. This feels different from a liability claim against the at-fault driver's insurer.

In theory, the dynamic should be different too. Your insurance company has contractual duties to you as their policyholder. They're supposed to deal with you in good faith and reach a fair resolution.

In practice, it doesn't always work that way. Many adjusters approach UM/UIM claims from an adversarial stance, treating them more like liability claims where their job is to minimize payout. This is frustrating, and it's arguably a violation of the duties they owe you. But it happens.

If your own insurance company is treating your UM/UIM claim unfairly, you have options—including potential bad faith claims against your insurer. We'll discuss insurance bad faith later in this book.

How UM/UIM Claims Go Wrong

When it comes to UM/UIM, there are several ways injured people leave money on the table.

Not making the claim at all. Some people don't realize they have UM/UIM coverage, or don't understand that it applies to their situation. They never file the claim.

Not claiming on other household policies. If your spouse has a separate auto policy, or your adult children living at home have their own policies, those might provide additional UM/UIM coverage for your accident. People often miss this.

The carrier applies an improper exclusion. The insurance company denies coverage based on an exclusion that isn't valid under New Mexico law. The policyholder accepts the denial without challenging it.

The carrier fails to recognize stacking. The insurance company calculates coverage based on a single vehicle when stacking should apply. The policyholder doesn't know to push back.

The carrier undervalues compensatory damages. The adjuster lowballs pain and suffering, lost wages, or other damages. The policyholder accepts less than the claim is worth.

The carrier ignores punitive damages. In cases involving reckless conduct, punitive damages should be part of the evaluation. Some carriers don't include them.

But the most common way UM/UIM claims go wrong happens before the accident ever occurs: you didn't buy UM/UIM coverage, or you didn't buy enough.

Common Surprises

People are often surprised that they need to make a claim on their own policy when someone else was at fault. It feels backwards. You didn't do anything wrong—why should your insurance have to pay?

But that's exactly why UM/UIM exists. It protects you when the person who hurt you can't or won't pay what they owe. It's coverage you bought precisely for this situation.

Another common concern: will making a UM/UIM claim raise my rates? By law, your rates should not increase because you made a UM/UIM claim. You're not at fault. You're using coverage you paid for because someone else failed to carry adequate insurance. That's not supposed to count against you.

But the biggest surprise—and the biggest regret—comes when people learn everything UM/UIM covers, how it works, how it might stack across multiple vehicles and policies, and realize they would have made very different purchasing decisions if they'd understood this from the beginning.

You can't go back and buy more coverage after an accident but if you believe you were misled during the original purchase, talk to a New Mexico insurance attorney about your options.

Key Takeaways

- UM coverage applies when the at-fault driver has no insurance or was never identified. UIM applies when their coverage isn't enough.
- UIM offsets mean the carrier subtracts the at-fault driver's liability limits from your UIM limits. $25k liability + $50k UIM = $50k total, not $75k.
- New Mexico has protective rules: technical requirements for selling UM/UIM, very few valid exclusions, and potential stacking across vehicles.
- You don't have to be in your insured vehicle to access UM/UIM. Passengers, bus riders, pedestrians, and even drive-by shooting victims have used it.
- UM/UIM covers everything liability would: medical bills, pain and suffering, lost income, property damage, and potentially punitive damages.
- Claims go wrong when people don't file, miss household policies, accept improper denials, or don't challenge undervaluation.
- Your rates should not increase from a UM/UIM claim.
- The biggest mistake happens before the accident: not buying UM/UIM or not buying enough.

CHAPTER 8

MEDICAL TREATMENT AND YOUR CLAIM

Medical treatment is at the heart of your injury claim. It's not just about getting better—though that matters most. Your treatment history is also the primary evidence of what happened to you, how badly you were hurt, and what you lost as a result.

Understanding the relationship between treatment and your claim helps you make better decisions about your care and avoid mistakes that could undermine your case.

How Treatment Affects What You Can Recover

New Mexico law allows injured people to recover damages in several categories. These come from the jury instructions that govern trials, but they also guide settlement negotiations at every stage. The categories include past and future medical expenses, past and future pain and suffering, past and future loss of enjoyment of life, the nature of the injury itself including disfigurement, and lost income.

Medical treatment figures into all of these, either directly or indirectly.

Medical expenses are straightforward. The cost of treatment—past bills and anticipated future care—is a direct component of damages.

Pain and suffering is harder to quantify. Medical treatment isn't the only measure of pain, but it's a widespread proxy. From a practical standpoint, more treatment is a rough indication that someone suffered more pain. That's not always perfectly true, but it's generally how adjusters, attorneys, and juries think about it.

Loss of enjoyment of life works similarly. More treatment suggests more disruption to your daily activities, your hobbies, your relationships. Treatment history becomes evidence of what you couldn't do while you were recovering.

Nature of the injury and disfigurement are also supported by treatment records. Surgeries, procedures, and ongoing care document the severity and lasting effects of what happened.

Lost income connects to treatment too. Your medical records help establish whether you could work during recovery, and for how long you were unable to earn a living.

The Threshold: Related, Necessary, and Reasonable

Not all medical treatment counts toward your claim. To figure into your damages, treatment must meet three criteria.

Related to the accident. The injury must have resulted from the collision or been aggravated—made worse—by it. Treatment for conditions unrelated to the accident doesn't count.

Necessary. The treatment must have been medically necessary as a result of your injury. Unnecessary procedures or excessive care don't contribute to your damages.

Reasonable. The cost must be reasonable for the treatment provided. If a single outpatient follow-up appointment costs $15,000, that's not reasonable, and it won't be counted at full value.

If your treatment is related, necessary, and reasonable, it supports your claim across all the damage categories. If it fails any of these tests, it becomes a problem.

Common Mistakes with Medical Treatment

People make predictable mistakes with their medical treatment that end up hurting their claims.

Waiting too long to seek treatment. This is the biggest one. People think their injuries will resolve on their own. They believe it's not that bad, or they can tough it out. Then things get worse, and they finally see a doctor—weeks or months after the accident.

That initial gap creates problems. The defense will argue that your injuries must have come from something else, not the accident. Or that you're exaggerating. Or that your sudden need for treatment was prompted by a lawyer getting involved, not by genuine injury.

If you're hurt, get checked out. If it's truly something minor that will resolve on its own, there's little harm in having had it evaluated. But if it turns out to be more serious, you'll be glad you went early.

Not following through on treatment. When you miss appointments, ignore your doctor's recommendations, or skip home exercises your physical therapist assigned, you undermine your case. The defense will point to your non-compliance and argue that you must not have been that injured, or that your failure to follow medical advice is why you're not better.

Follow doctor's orders. Do the exercises. Show up for appointments. This matters for your health and for your claim.

Gaps in treatment. Sometimes people treat for a while, start feeling better, stop treatment, and then get worse again. This happens—healing isn't linear. But gaps in your treatment history create obstacles.

Depending on the circumstances and the size of the case, we may bring in pain specialists or other experts to explain why the gap occurred. But it's not ideal. If you're still experiencing symptoms, keep treating. If your doctor says you can stop, document that it was their recommendation.

Choosing Providers

Even though this is an accident case, you're often still relying on your regular health insurance to pay for treatment before your case settles. That means your choices are constrained by your insurance network—whether you can go straight to a specialist depends on your plan, your HMO rules, and your referral requirements.

Navigating health insurance could fill its own book. But the advice I give is simple: follow your primary care doctor's recommendations for follow-up care, specialists, and referrals. Let them guide you through the system. If they recommend a specialist, see that specialist. If they recommend physical therapy, do physical therapy.

Don't try to engineer your treatment choices around what you think will help your claim. Get the care you need, when you need it, from the providers your doctor recommends.

Your Medical Records Will Be Used

Everything you say to medical providers can end up in your records. Those records will be reviewed by insurance adjusters, by attorneys, and potentially by a jury. Keep that in mind.

Be honest about everything. Don't try to manipulate the system through what you tell your doctors. The things people do to game the system usually hurt them more than they help.

Some intake forms ask directly: is this the result of an accident? Be honest. Think about what checking "no" will mean later when your medical records are reviewed. I don't know why people check "no" when they were injured in an accident—maybe concern about insurance rates—but it creates a problem for your claim.

If a provider makes an incorrect note, try to get it corrected. Medical records sometimes contain errors. Maybe the doctor wrote down the wrong date, or recorded a symptom you didn't report, or got the mechanism of injury wrong. If you notice an error, point it out and ask for a correction. It doesn't always happen, but it's important to try.

The bottom line: be as honest and forthcoming as you can at every stage, and let the chips fall where they do. Honesty protects you better than any attempt to manage the narrative.

Pre-Existing Conditions

What if you had back problems before the accident, and the accident made them worse? Pre-existing conditions complicate things, but they don't eliminate your claim.

Under New Mexico law, you can still recover damages for the extent to which the accident aggravated a preexisting condition. If you had a bad back that was manageable before the crash and now requires surgery, the aggravation is compensable—even though you weren't starting from perfect health.

The challenge is figuring out how much of your current condition is pre-existing and how much resulted from the accident. In cases that justify it, we use medical experts to sort this out.

Here's how the principle works. Say you received $20,000 in treatment. Medical testimony establishes that your pre-existing condition accounted for 40% of your need for care, and the accident-related aggravation accounted for 60%. In that scenario, $12,000 would be attributable to your claim.

It rarely works out that neatly in real cases, but that's the concept. Pre-existing conditions don't bar recovery—they just require careful analysis of what the accident caused.

Be upfront about your medical history with both your providers and your attorney. Hiding a preexisting condition is far worse than disclosing it. Your attorney needs to know so they can address it properly.

Remember that if the claim goes to litigation, the attorneys on the other side can usually obtain medical records spanning years before the accident.

Keep Good Records

One practical thing you can do to help your case: keep track of which providers and clinics you've visited. Names, addresses, dates of appointments.

Your attorney's office will need to gather all your medical records and bills to build your claim. Having a clear list of where you've been makes this process faster and reduces the chance that something gets missed.

You don't need to do anything elaborate. A simple list on your phone or a piece of paper works fine. Just note each provider as you go.

Key Takeaways

- Medical treatment directly affects your claim's value. It's evidence of medical expenses, pain and suffering, lost enjoyment of life, the nature of your injury, and lost income.
- Treatment must be related to the accident, necessary, and reasonable to count toward damages.
- Don't wait to seek treatment after an accident. Gaps between the accident and first treatment create problems.
- Follow through on treatment. Missed appointments and ignored recommendations undermine your case.
- Be honest with your medical providers. Don't try to game intake forms or manipulate records.
- Pre-existing conditions don't bar your claim. You can recover for the extent the accident made things worse.
- Keep a list of every provider and clinic you visit. It helps your attorney gather what's needed.

CHAPTER 9

GETTING YOUR BILLS PAID WHILE YOUR CASE IS PENDING

Your case might take months to resolve. It might take years. Meanwhile, medical bills arrive in the mail. Providers want to be paid. Collection agencies start calling.

This is one of the most stressful parts of an injury claim—managing your financial obligations while waiting for a settlement that hasn't happened yet. This chapter explains your options and what you need to understand about how bills get handled.

There's No Single Timeline

People always want to know how long their case will take. The honest answer is that it depends.

Several factors affect the timeline. How severe are your injuries? How long does treatment take? How cooperative is the insurance company? How backed up are the courts? What are the policy limits at issue?

Sometimes cases resolve quickly. If you have a serious injury that exceeds the at-fault driver's policy limits, the insurance company may offer those limits right away because liability and damages are so obvious. There's no point in fighting.

But even a small claim can drag on for years if the insurance company decides to contest it. A carrier that disputes liability or questions your injuries can stretch things out through negotiation, litigation, and appeals.

Plan for your case to take longer than you'd like. Hope for faster, but don't count on it.

Options for Paying Medical Bills

While your case is pending, you have a few ways to handle medical expenses.

Health insurance. If you have health insurance through an employer, the marketplace, or a government program, use it. This is typically the best first option. Your health insurance will pay for accident-related treatment just like it pays for any other medical care.

There's a catch, which we'll discuss in a moment. But for now, understand that health insurance is usually the most practical way to get treatment while your case is pending.

Medical payments coverage. If you have med pay coverage on your auto policy, it can pay medical bills up to a certain limit—typically around $5,000, though amounts vary. This coverage pays regardless of who was at fault in the accident.

Med pay can be useful, but there's a trade-off. Health insurance plans have negotiated contractual rates with in-network providers.

When you use health insurance, you get those lower rates. Medical payments coverage doesn't have those arrangements. The same treatment might be billed at a higher rate when it goes through med pay.

Sometimes hospitals or clinics will ask you to sign paperwork allowing them to bill your med pay coverage directly. They prefer this because they get paid their full charges instead of the lower negotiated rates they'd receive from a health insurer. Be aware of this dynamic.

Letters of protection. Some providers are willing to treat you now and wait for payment until your case settles. This arrangement is typically documented in a "letter of protection"—a letter from your attorney promising to pay the provider from your settlement in exchange for treatment.

Not all providers work this way. Chiropractors and some physical therapists often accept letters of protection. Most hospitals, surgeons, and other medical providers do not. They want to be paid through insurance or up front.

Letters of protection can help you access treatment when you don't have other options. But understand that the bills are accumulating, and they'll come out of your settlement at the end.

Subrogation: The Surprise That Catches People

Here's something that surprises many people. If your health insurance pays for accident-related treatment, they expect to be paid back from your settlement.

This is called subrogation. It's a long-standing legal principle that applies in most states, including New Mexico. The concept is straightforward: if an at-fault party caused the insurance company to pay for your medical care, the insurance company has a right to recover that money from whatever you collect from the at-fault party.

When your case settles, your health insurer will assert a subrogation claim. They'll want reimbursement for what they paid.

The good news is that subrogation claims are often negotiable. For various legal reasons, the amount the health insurer can recover is not necessarily dollar-for-dollar what they paid. There are opportunities to reduce the subrogation amount. But the health insurer does have a right to recover something.

This means your settlement won't all be yours to keep. A portion will go back to your health insurance company to reimburse them for accident-related care.

Liens Work Similarly

Sometimes a hospital or clinic will provide treatment and file a lien on your case rather than billing your insurance. A lien is a legal claim against your settlement—the provider is saying they're owed money from whatever you recover.

Like subrogation, liens get paid from your settlement at the end of the case. The provider waits for payment, but they have a legally enforceable right to collect.

If a provider files a lien, your attorney needs to know about it so it can be addressed when the case resolves.

Medicare Has Special Rules

If you have Medicare, pay close attention. Medicare has its own rules about injury claims, and the consequences for not following them can be serious.

Medicare is entitled to be repaid from your settlement or judgment for any accident-related treatment they covered. This is federal law, and it's strictly enforced.

Medicare may also require a "set-aside"—money from your settlement that gets reserved for future accident-related medical treatment. The rules around Medicare set-asides are complex and depend on the specifics of your case.

If you have Medicare, give your attorney a copy of your Medicare card early. They need to report the claim to Medicare, track conditional payments, and make sure everything is handled in compliance with federal requirements. This is not optional.

Medicaid in New Mexico

In New Mexico, Medicaid is administered through private insurance carriers who receive funding from the government. From your perspective as a patient, it functions similarly to marketplace or employer-provided health insurance.

That includes subrogation. If Medicaid pays for your accident-related treatment, they have the same right to reimbursement from your settlement that a private health insurer would have.

The discussion of subrogation above generally applies to Medicaid as well. Let your attorney know if you have Medicaid coverage so they can handle it appropriately.

Medicare Advantage Plans

If you're on a Medicare Advantage plan—a private plan that provides your Medicare benefits—your attorney needs to know. Medicare Advantage plans can have different rules and requirements that affect how your case is handled.

Don't assume your attorney will know what coverage you have. Tell them, and provide documentation.

Don't Ignore Your Bills

While your case is pending, don't simply ignore medical bills that arrive. Unpaid bills can go to collections, and that can affect your credit—even though you're expecting a settlement that will eventually cover them.

New Mexico has enacted some protections around medical debt collection and reporting. Laws like the Surprise Billing Act have changed some of the rules around how medical debt is handled. The details are beyond the scope of this book, but the protections exist.

If you receive a collection notice for accident-related medical bills, let your attorney know. There may be steps they can take, or information they can provide to the collector, to address the situation while your case is pending.

The important thing is not to just throw the notices away and hope for the best. Stay on top of it and keep your attorney informed.

This Is Technical—Let Your Attorney Handle It

The interplay between medical bills, health insurance payments, and subrogation claims is more complicated than it might seem.

Here's an example of the complexity. For any given treatment, there are usually three numbers: the amount the provider charged, the amount the health insurance company paid (after contractual adjustments), and the amount the health insurer claims they're entitled to in subrogation. These are often all different.

Sorting this out requires gathering specific records—explanation of benefits statements, billing records, payment histories. Then there's an opportunity to negotiate reductions in subrogation claims, which can put more money in your pocket.

This is something attorneys handle routinely, sometimes working with specialized vendors who focus on subrogation resolution. It's also something that people who handle claims on their own can easily miss or mishandle.

If you're working with an attorney, let them manage this. If you're handling your claim yourself, understand that this is one of the areas where professional help adds real value.

Key Takeaways

- There's no single timeline for injury claims. Cases can resolve in months or drag on for years depending on many factors.
- Options for paying bills while your case is pending include health insurance, medical payments coverage from your auto policy, and letters of protection with certain providers.
- Health insurance typically results in lower costs because of negotiated rates. Med pay doesn't have those discounts.
- Subrogation means your health insurer expects to be repaid from your settlement. This is negotiable but unavoidable.

- Liens work similarly—providers who file liens get paid from your recovery.
- Medicare has strict federal rules about repayment and potential set-asides. Give your attorney your Medicare card early.
- Medicaid in New Mexico follows similar subrogation rules as private insurance.
- Don't ignore bills while your case is pending. Collections can still happen. Keep your attorney informed.
- This area is technical. Professional help makes a difference in getting it right.

CHAPTER 10

PROPERTY DAMAGE

When your car gets damaged in an accident, you want it fixed or replaced. This chapter explains how property damage claims work, what your options are, and how to avoid leaving money on the table.

Property Damage Is Separate from Your Injury Claim

Property damage can and should be handled separately from your bodily injury claim. In fact, property damage is often resolved within the first few weeks after an accident, while the injury claim may take months or years.

New Mexico law prohibits insurance companies from using one type of claim to leverage an outcome on the other. They can't pressure you to settle your injury claim by holding up your property damage payment, or vice versa.

The connection between property damage and bodily injury is only indirect. For example, if your car is totaled, that suggests a certain level of impact and force. A demolished vehicle can help substantiate claims of severe injuries. But the two claims are handled through separate processes.

When Your Car Is a Total Loss

A vehicle is deemed a total loss when it's uneconomical to repair. If the cost to repair plus the salvage value exceeds the vehicle's pre-accident actual cash value, it's totaled.

You typically don't get a say in whether your car is declared a total loss. The insurance company makes that determination based on their valuation of your vehicle's pre-accident worth and the repair estimates from body shops. If you believe their numbers are wrong, you can seek estimates from your own shops and challenge the valuation.

One thing that surprises people: total loss doesn't mean inoperable. A car with extensive body damage but no underlying mechanical problems might run just fine—and still be a total loss. The determination is purely about economics, not whether the vehicle can drive.

Here's something important to understand about New Mexico law. Once a car is deemed a total loss, it becomes a salvage vehicle by law. It cannot be registered to drive on public highways until you provide proof of repair to MVD.

This matters if you're thinking about keeping the salvage because the car "still runs fine." You can't simply pocket the insurance payout and keep driving without getting repairs done and cleared through MVD. Factor that into your decision.

What Happens After a Total Loss

If your car is totaled and you don't retain the salvage, the insurance company typically turns the vehicle over to an auction lot. It gets auctioned off, and you'll have no idea where it ends up.

Usually, that's fine. You've been paid for the vehicle's value, and you have no further use for a wrecked car.

But in a small set of cases, losing control of the vehicle means losing critical evidence.

If you have catastrophic injuries, there may be questions later about the mechanics of the crash—how the vehicles collided, what forces were involved, what caused what. If there's a significant punitive damages claim, the condition of the vehicles might be relevant evidence. If there are allegations of product liability—something wrong with the car itself contributed to the accident or your injuries—the vehicle is essential evidence.

Once the salvage is auctioned, it's gone. You can't get it back for inspection or expert analysis.

In these situations, it sometimes makes sense to retain the salvage even though it reduces your payout. Talk to your attorney about whether this applies to your case before you let the vehicle go.

Three Coverages That Might Apply

When you're dealing with property damage, your claim might fall under one of three coverages.

The at-fault driver's liability coverage. If someone else caused the accident and they have insurance, their liability policy should pay for your vehicle damage. But this requires a fault determination, which can take time.

Your own collision coverage. This is typically the first stop. Collision coverage applies regardless of who was at fault. Because no fault investigation is necessary—all that matters is your vehicle's value and the cost to repair—your insurance company should handle this quickly. If they don't, there's a problem.

Your own UM/UIM coverage. This comes into play in uninsured, underinsured, or hit-and-run situations. For example, many liability policies have property damage limits of only $10,000. But plenty of vehicles are worth more than that, and repair costs can easily exceed $10,000 even without totaling the car. That's an underinsured situation where your UM/UIM coverage applies.

How Collision Coverage and Subrogation Work

If your own collision coverage pays for your vehicle damage, your insurance company has the option to pursue subrogation against the at-fault driver's carrier. They'll try to recover what they paid you from the other driver's insurance.

This is often handled through inter-company arbitration or simple negotiation between the insurers. You typically don't have to be involved. If it goes smoothly, you may just receive a check for your deductible and not have to think about property damage again.

UM/UIM Covers More Than Collision

Here's something many people don't realize. UM/UIM property damage coverage includes categories of damages that collision coverage doesn't cover.

Loss of use. This refers to the time you didn't have use of your vehicle—while it was in the shop for repairs, for example. You're entitled to compensation for that lost use, typically calculated by reference to what it would cost to rent a similar vehicle.

Punitive damages. If the at-fault driver's conduct was reckless—like driving drunk—punitive damages may be available. Your UM/UIM carrier has to include punitive damages in their evaluation. There's no formula for calculating them, and it often becomes a point of dispute, but they should be part of the conversation.

Diminished value. Even after your vehicle is fully repaired, a car with a collision in its history is worth less than one without. It won't sell for as much as it would have before the accident. You're entitled to that difference, called diminished value or diminution of value.

Many adjusters will try to close out a property damage claim after collision coverage pays, without ever addressing UM/UIM. In the right circumstances, that leaves significant money on the table.

An Example: The Uninsured Drunk Driver

Let's walk through a scenario to show how this works.

An uninsured drunk driver collides with your vehicle and causes $15,000 in damage. Your car is worth $30,000, so it's not a total loss. You have collision coverage with a $1,000 deductible and UM/UIM coverage with $50,000 in property damage limits.

Your collision coverage pays $14,000—the damages minus your deductible. You pay the remaining $1,000 out of pocket and have the vehicle repaired. The car is in the shop for ten days.

Many adjusters will try to end the claim right there. Don't let them.

In this situation, you should push for a UM/UIM evaluation. Why? Because there's more money available in four ways.

Punitive damages. The at-fault driver was intoxicated. That's a classic case for punitive damages.

Loss of use. Your vehicle was in the shop for ten days. You're entitled to the reasonable value of a day's use of a comparable vehicle for each of those days.

Diminished value. Your repaired vehicle is now worth less than it was before the accident because of the collision history. You're entitled to that difference.

Deductible recovery. By law, UM/UIM property damage coverage in New Mexico has a $250 deductible—lower than most collision deductibles. The UM/UIM coverage should make up the $750 difference between your $1,000 collision deductible and the $250 UM/UIM deductible.

Depending on the circumstances, failing to pursue UM/UIM evaluation could mean leaving thousands of dollars on the table.

Rental Cars While Your Vehicle Is Out

If your car is being repaired or you're waiting for a total loss payout, you probably need transportation. How do rental cars work?

Most collision coverage policies are sold with rental reimbursement for a limited time period. Check your policy to see what you have. The coverage typically pays for a rental car while your vehicle is in the shop or while the total loss claim is being processed.

Your insurance company may have deals with certain rental car companies. They may even make the reservation for you and pay the rental company directly. This sounds convenient, but it can lead to miscommunications.

I've seen situations where a rental vehicle was reported stolen because the insurance company dropped the ball on renewing the reservation and paying for it. The rental company didn't get paid, the reservation lapsed, and suddenly there's a stolen vehicle report with your name on it.

Protect yourself. Stay on top of things. Keep communicating with both your insurance company and the rental company. Don't assume everything is being handled just because someone said it would be.

Common Mistakes with Property Damage

The most common mistake people make with property damage claims is not getting their own independent estimates.

Insurance companies tend to have preferred body shops. These shops are "preferred" because they keep estimates lower. That's good for the insurance company's bottom line. It's not necessarily good for you.

Get your own estimates from shops you choose. If the insurance company's estimate seems low, you have something to compare it to.

Also, if more damage is discovered during the repair process—which happens frequently—make sure you get supplemental estimates. The initial estimate might not have accounted for damage that only becomes visible once the car is taken apart.

Advocate for yourself. Don't just accept whatever number the insurance company's preferred shop provides.

Attorneys and Property Damage

Here's something that might surprise you. It's typical for people to handle their own property damage claims even while they're represented by an attorney on the bodily injury side.

Why? Because property damage claims are more straightforward. They often don't depend on fault determinations. And most importantly, you don't necessarily want an attorney taking a percentage of the property damage recovery. If you need $14,000 to repair your car and an attorney takes a third, you're left without enough money to actually do the repairs.

Some attorneys will help with property damage without taking a fee from that portion of the recovery. If your attorney offers to help, clarify whether they're charging for it. Be clear about what's happening.

I typically only get involved with a client's property damage claim if there's evidence of insurance bad faith or improper claims handling—situations where we need to make a bigger issue of it than just the damage itself.

This might arise if, for example, the insurance company is refusing to do a UM/UIM evaluation on the grounds that the claim was already handled through collision. Or if there's a clear punitive damages claim that the adjuster is refusing to value or is seriously undervaluing. Those situations may require attorney involvement to get resolved properly.

For straightforward property damage, though, you can often handle it yourself—even if you have an attorney for your injury claim.

Key Takeaways

- Property damage is separate from your injury claim and can usually be resolved quickly.
- A car is a total loss when repair cost plus salvage value exceeds pre-accident value. In New Mexico, a totaled car becomes a

salvage vehicle and can't be driven until repairs are cleared through MVD.
- Three coverages might apply: the at-fault driver's liability, your collision coverage, or your UM/UIM coverage.
- Collision coverage is usually the fastest route—no fault determination needed.
- UM/UIM covers things collision doesn't: loss of use, punitive damages, diminished value, and deductible differences.
- In uninsured or underinsured situations, push for UM/UIM evaluation. Don't let adjusters close the claim after collision pays.
- Get your own repair estimates. Insurance company preferred shops tend to estimate low.
- Stay on top of rental car arrangements. Miscommunications happen.
- You may handle property damage yourself even while represented on the injury claim. Clarify with your attorney whether they're helping and whether they're charging.
- In cases involving catastrophic injuries, punitive damages, or product liability, consider retaining the salvage as evidence before it's auctioned off.

CHAPTER 11

WHAT YOUR CASE IS WORTH

Everyone wants to know what their case is worth. It's the first question most people ask, and it's completely understandable. You've been hurt. You're dealing with medical bills, lost wages, pain, and disruption to your life. You want to know what you can expect.

Here's the honest answer: your case is worth whatever a jury will award for it.

That's true, but it's not particularly helpful. So let's dig deeper into how case valuation actually works.

The Categories of Damages

New Mexico law allows injured people to recover damages in several categories. These come from the jury instructions that govern trials, but they also guide how attorneys and insurance companies evaluate cases at every stage.

Compensatory damages are meant to compensate you for what you lost. They include:

- Past and future medical expenses. What you've already spent on treatment and what you'll need to spend going forward.
- Past and future non-medical expenses caused by the injury. Out-of-pocket costs like transportation to medical appointments, home modifications, or equipment you needed because of your injuries.
- Past and future pain and suffering. The physical pain you've experienced and will continue to experience.
- Past and future loss of enjoyment of life. The activities, hobbies, and pleasures you can no longer participate in because of your injuries.
- The nature of the injury, including disfigurement. Scarring, amputation, or other permanent changes to your body.
- Lost income or wages. Money you didn't earn because you couldn't work.
- Loss of future earning potential. If your injuries affect your ability to earn money going forward, that diminished capacity is compensable.
- Loss of household services. If you can't do chores around the house that you used to do, that has value too.

Additionally, spouses and children may have related claims for loss of consortium—damages to the relationship caused by your injuries.

Punitive damages are different. They're not meant to compensate you. They're meant to punish the at-fault party for particularly bad conduct. Punitive damages may be available when there was reckless, malicious, wanton, or willful behavior. In the car accident context, drunk driving is the classic example.

Objective and Subjective Damages

Some of these damage categories are objective. They can be documented and calculated.

Medical expenses are based on what was billed in the past and what a medical expert will say is reasonably necessary in the future. Out-of-pocket expenses are shown by receipts and invoices. Past lost wages are documented through paystubs showing missed work and your typical wage or salary. Household services are typically valued at a modest hourly rate multiplied by the time you couldn't perform them.

These numbers can be pinned down through documentation.

Other categories are more subjective. Pain and suffering, loss of enjoyment of life, and damages for the nature of your injury or disfigurement—these are harder to quantify. They're about telling the story of how your injuries have affected your life.

Photographs help. Medical records documenting your condition help. Statements from family and friends who can describe the changes they've witnessed help. The goal is to paint a picture that a jury can understand and connect with.

A word of caution: decision-makers—judges and juries—don't like complainers or people who appear to be milking their case. Be honest and be reasonable. Exaggeration backfires.

The Reference Point Problem

Because the subjective damages are hard to pin down, everyone tends to evaluate them relative to the objective measures. Medical costs become the reference point.

This isn't right for every case. Sometimes people suffer enormously even with relatively low medical bills. A person with chronic pain who manages it through lifestyle changes rather than expensive procedures has still suffered. But in those cases, the qualitative evidence must be especially compelling.

If your medical bills are modest but your suffering is significant, you'll need to work harder to document and communicate the impact on your life.

Similar Cases Matter

The final ingredient in valuation is looking at settlements and verdicts from similar cases.

What have juries awarded for comparable injuries? What have similar cases settled for? This information helps establish a reasonable range.

Your attorney should have experience with similar cases and access to verdict and settlement databases. They may also consult with other attorneys to gut-check their own valuations—without revealing confidential information about your case.

The key is taking all this information—the documented damages, the subjective impacts, the comparable outcomes—and compiling it into a reasonable narrative that points to a reasonable range of values.

The Biggest Misconception

The biggest misconception about case value is that people think their case is worth much more than it is.

The cases that make the news do so because they're rare, unusual, and noteworthy. And often, the severity of the injuries isn't fully reported. What you read in the headlines is often misinformation. The true facts of these cases are very different from what gets covered in the media.

Here's reality. Death, paralysis, around-the-clock home care, traumatic brain injuries resulting in severe impairment, inability to walk, or inability to work—these are the injuries that result in large verdicts or settlements.

If you haven't suffered something like this, be grateful that your injuries were not worse. And adjust your expectations accordingly.

The Insurance Cap

Here's another reality that limits case value: your potential recovery is usually capped at the amount of available insurance.

Sometimes that's not true. When the at-fault party is a business or someone with significant personal assets, there may be more to recover. But that's rare.

In the overwhelming majority of cases, the insurance is the maximum. If the available insurance is $25,000, that's the most you're going to get—no matter how badly you were injured.

This is why we spend time early in the case identifying all possible sources of insurance coverage. It's also why your own UM/UIM coverage matters so much. The at-fault driver's policy might not be enough.

What You Can Do to Help

Outside of catastrophic cases, the best thing you can do to help establish the true value of your case is to help gather the information your attorney needs to tell a compelling story.

Get your attorney in touch with family members and friends who can validate changes in your lifestyle. Help them understand who you were before the accident and who you are now.

Talk about hobbies you used to enjoy but can't anymore. Describe activities that are now difficult or impossible. Document how your daily life has changed.

Your attorney can compile the medical records and bills. But you're the one who can bring the human story to life.

Demand vs. Valuation

One thing people should understand: the first number we put forward—the demand—is not the valuation of your case.

The demand is a high figure that gives us room to negotiate. If I suggest an initial demand of $100,000, that means I think a fair settlement for the case is likely somewhere between $40,000 and $60,000.

The insurance company will respond with a low number—maybe $10,000. Then we negotiate from there, each side moving toward a reasonable compromise.

Don't confuse the demand with what your case is worth. The demand is a negotiating position.

Why Pushing Longer Can Increase Offers

Generally, the longer we stay in the fight, the more the insurance company will offer. There are two reasons for this.

First, time in litigation clarifies the facts. As we take depositions, gather evidence, and work up the case, everyone learns more about what actually happened and what a trial might look like. The perceived range of possible outcomes narrows. That pushes both sides toward compromise.

Second, litigation costs money. As the case goes on, both sides incur attorney fees and case costs—especially expert witness fees. At some point, the cost of continuing to fight tips the balance toward offering a reasonable settlement.

Diminishing Returns

That said, there's a point of diminishing returns.

Sometimes we reach a crossroads where the conversation with the client looks like this: the insurance company has offered X. The next stage in litigation is to hire expert witnesses—maybe multiple experts—to make our case at trial. That's going to cost Y.

Good testimony from our experts might increase their offer. But if the increase is approximately Y, what have we gained? We've spent the additional money just to end up in roughly the same place.

These are judgment calls. They depend on the specific facts of your case, the amount at stake, and your own appetite for continued litigation.

How Attorneys Approach Valuation

When you ask an attorney what your case is worth, the conversation involves many questions.

What treatment have you received? Did you miss work? What have the doctors told you about your diagnoses? What are they recommending for the future? Did you require surgery? Tell me how this has impacted your life. What activities did you previously enjoy that are now difficult or impossible? What's your pain like on a daily basis?

The attorney takes your answers, combines them with the documented evidence, compares the situation to similar cases they've handled or researched, and arrives at a range.

There's no formula. But an experienced attorney should be able to give you a sense of what similar cases have settled for.

The Fundamental Uncertainty

Here's the most important thing to understand about case valuation: we don't know.

We simply don't know what might happen at trial. We don't know what a jury—twelve people chosen essentially at random from the public—might think about your case and your injuries.

Think about the makeup of a jury. Jury selection isn't really "picking a jury." We don't get to decide who decides your case. Jury selection is really about identifying and keeping extremists off the panel. What you end up with is twelve essentially unremarkable people.

They could be very liberal or very conservative. Someone might philosophically oppose punitive damages. Someone else might have been in an accident and gotten nothing, making them skeptical of injury claims. Another might have never dealt with insurance and have no perspective. They could be eighteen years old or eighty. Scientists or high school dropouts.

This uncertainty is irreducible. No one can tell you exactly what a jury will do.

Tools to Reduce Uncertainty

There are ways to get a better picture of what a jury might do with your case. Focus groups and mock juries allow you to present a distilled version of your case to people with various backgrounds and collect their opinions.

This has become more accessible now that it can be done through video conferencing. It's actually possible to get hundreds of people from all sorts of backgrounds to react to your case and provide useful data. Done well, it can give a reasonably good prediction of trial outcomes.

But here's the catch: this is extremely expensive. We're talking tens of thousands of dollars. And that's a case cost that comes out of your settlement.

Focus groups and mock juries only make sense when the injuries and the available insurance justify the expense. In most cases, they don't.

What You're Left With

For the majority of cases, you're working from your attorney's background experience and their consultations with other attorneys who handle similar matters.

It's not a crystal ball. It's informed judgment based on years of handling cases, knowledge of what similar situations have settled for, and an understanding of how juries in New Mexico tend to respond.

Your attorney should be able to give you a reasonable range. But understand that it's a range, not a guarantee. The uncertainty is built into the system.

Key Takeaways

- New Mexico law allows recovery for medical expenses, lost wages, pain and suffering, loss of enjoyment of life, disfigurement, and more. Punitive damages may be available for reckless conduct.
- Some damages are objective and documentable. Others are subjective and require telling your story effectively.
- The biggest misconception is that cases are worth more than they are. Large verdicts involve catastrophic injuries. Media coverage is often misleading.
- Recovery is usually capped at available insurance. A $25,000 policy means $25,000 maximum, regardless of injury severity.
- The demand is not the valuation—it's a negotiating position. Expect the final number to be significantly lower than the initial demand.
- Pushing longer in litigation can increase offers, but there's a point of diminishing returns when costs outweigh gains.
- Jury outcomes are fundamentally uncertain. Twelve random people will decide your case, and no one can predict exactly what they'll do.
- Help your attorney tell a compelling story by connecting them with people who can validate how your life has changed.

CHAPTER 12
NEGOTIATING A SETTLEMENT

Most car accident cases settle. They don't go to trial. They don't result in a dramatic verdict. Instead, sometime in the process, the two sides reach an agreement, paperwork gets signed, and a check arrives.

Understanding how settlement negotiation works helps you participate meaningfully in the process and set realistic expectations about what's happening and why.

Pre-Litigation Negotiation

Before a lawsuit is filed, you're typically dealing with a liability adjuster at the insurance company. That adjuster is often located out of state, handling hundreds of files simultaneously.

Insurance companies don't evaluate cases the way you might expect. They use tools and algorithms—proprietary databases, either built in-house or licensed from third-party companies. The adjuster inputs certain information, like liability assessments and medical treatment codes, and the system generates a "value" for the case.

This process is impersonal. It doesn't account for qualitative factors—how your injuries have actually affected your life, the specific circumstances of your accident, the story behind the numbers. The data the system relies on may be imperfect or biased.

This is what asymmetry looks like. Insurance companies have spent decades and billions of dollars building systems to process claims efficiently—which, from their perspective, means paying less. You're bringing a pen to what is increasingly a data fight.

The adjuster on the other end of the phone isn't your adversary in the way you might think. They're a person doing a difficult job inside a system designed to constrain them. They're monitored, measured on metrics, and juggling more files than any one person can meaningfully manage. Fifty years ago, adjusters were professionals with real discretion—investigators who evaluated claims and made judgment calls. Today, they're increasingly babysitting files that are scored and valued by opaque automated processes. The algorithm suggests a number. The adjuster's job is to defend it.

This matters for how you think about negotiation. If the person across the table has limited authority to deviate from what the system says, human-to-human persuasion only goes so far. Moving the needle often requires action—usually litigation—that changes the inputs the system is weighing. It's not about convincing the adjuster. It's about changing the calculus.

In terms of pure mechanics, pre-litigation negotiation is straightforward. Your attorney makes a demand. The insurance company responds with an offer. Then it's back and forth—counter-offers until you either reach a resolution or decide you're not making progress.

The Only Real Leverage

If pre-litigation negotiation stalls, the only real leverage your attorney has is to sue.

Filing a lawsuit changes the dynamic. It signals that you're serious about pursuing the case. It starts a clock running. It creates costs and pressures that didn't exist before.

But here's something important to understand: a lawsuit does not equal a trial.

When your attorney files a lawsuit—initiated by a document called a complaint that causes the court to open an official record with a case number—trial could still be years away. There are many opportunities to reach a settlement between filing suit and actually walking into a courtroom.

Filing a lawsuit is a step in the process, not the end of the process.

How Litigation Changes Negotiation

Once a lawsuit is filed, negotiations look different.

You're typically no longer dealing with the same out-of-state adjuster who handled the pre-litigation file. Now there's a local defense attorney on the other side—someone hired by the insurance company to represent their insured. That attorney reports to an adjuster, often a different one than before.

Defense costs for the insurance company start accruing immediately. The defense attorney gets paid by the hour. Every motion, every deposition, every piece of discovery costs the insurance company money.

You also gain access to evidence through the discovery process. You can take depositions—sworn testimony from witnesses, the other driver, even the insurance company's representatives. Information that was hidden before becomes available.

The court may order the parties to attend mediation—a structured settlement conference designed to encourage resolution.

The fundamental mechanics remain the same: offers and counter-offers. But the pressures on the insurance company have escalated significantly.

What Mediation Looks Like

Mediation is a settlement process that typically happens over a day or half a day. A neutral third party—the mediator—acts as an intermediary between the two sides, trying to facilitate an agreement.

Mediators are often retired judges who bring real courtroom experience to the table. They've seen thousands of cases. They can offer feedback and reality checks to both sides based on what they've witnessed over their careers.

Here's how it works. Everyone gathers—the attorneys, their clients, and insurance representatives. But the two sides don't sit in the same room negotiating face to face. Instead, each side goes to a separate room. These might be physical conference rooms in the same building, or they might be virtual rooms on a video call.

The mediator moves back and forth between the rooms, carrying information and offers. They'll share what the other side is proposing, provide their own assessment of the strengths and weaknesses of each position, and try to guide both parties toward a middle ground.

The advantage of mediation is speed. Offers and counter-offers happen within minutes or hours rather than days or weeks. A negotiation that might have taken months through letters and phone calls can potentially be resolved in a single day.

Mediation doesn't always result in settlement. But it often does, and even when it doesn't, it usually moves the parties closer together.

Evaluating Whether an Offer Is Reasonable

When a settlement offer comes in, how do you know if it's fair?

I advise clients based on the factors we discussed in the previous chapter. The best guidance I can give is whether I believe the offer is fair compared to similar cases. What have other people with comparable injuries received? How does this offer stack up?

More than anything, I want my clients to receive a fair shake. I don't want to help people milk a case inappropriately—that's not who I am. But I also don't want them to be undercompensated for real injuries and real losses.

Different attorneys have different philosophies. Some care most about resolving cases quickly and handling a large volume. Some want to push every case as hard as possible, hoping to maximize recovery. That second approach sounds appealing, but it increases costs and increases risks.

I care most about fairness. If I feel like I got my client a fair result—in the mix with other people in similar situations—I rest easy with the job I did.

The Easy Versus Hard Framework

Here's how I often explain settlement offers to clients.

The other side—the insurance company—can make things easy or make things hard.

They make things easy by offering a lowball number. A clearly inadequate offer is easy to reject. You don't have to agonize over it. The answer is obviously no, and we keep negotiating or move toward litigation.

They also make things easy by offering a high figure—typically at or near the policy limits when there's a coverage cap. A near-maximum offer is easy to accept. You know you're getting most of what's available, and saying yes is straightforward.

They make things hard by offering a number in the middle. A middle-ground offer creates conflicting feelings. You wonder if you could do better. You also fear you could do worse. You're not sure whether to accept, reject, or counter.

If you're experiencing those conflicting feelings—simultaneously pulled toward yes and toward no—it probably means you're in the neighborhood of a true compromise position. Neither side is thrilled, but neither side is being treated unfairly.

Your attorney can offer guidance, but ultimately this is the client's decision to make.

It's Not Just About the Money

Settlement decisions aren't purely about case value. They're also about your goals and your risk tolerance.

Some clients just want to close this chapter of their lives. They're tired of dealing with the accident, the insurance company, the legal process. Getting a fair offer and moving on has real value to them, even if pushing harder might yield a bit more money.

Some clients want their day in court. They want to tell their story to a jury. They want accountability. They're willing to accept the risk of a bad result for the chance at vindication.

Most clients fall somewhere in between. They just want to know they've been treated fairly.

There's no single right answer. The right settlement depends on who you are and what matters to you.

Negotiations Can Always Restart

Settlement talks can stall. You might reach an impasse where neither side is willing to move. It can feel like the negotiation is over.

But negotiations can almost always restart. Negotiations are not concluded until you have signed a settlement agreement or the case has been fully litigated to conclusion, including all appeals and all collection efforts.

Even during trial, the parties can negotiate. Even after a verdict, while an appeal is pending, settlement discussions can happen. The case isn't truly over until it's over.

What changes is the context. Events during litigation—depositions that go well or poorly, rulings from the judge, the approach of a trial date—influence the range of values that both sides are willing to consider. A settlement that wasn't possible six months ago might become possible after new information emerges.

Keep this in mind if negotiations seem to have hit a wall. The wall might not be permanent.

Common Mistakes in Negotiation

People make predictable mistakes during settlement negotiations that can hurt their outcomes.

Rushing to the bottom line. Some people want to skip the back-and-forth and just get to the final number. This isn't how attorneys and insurance companies approach negotiation. If you rush to your bottom line, the other side will simply negotiate against that number—treating it as your opening position rather than your final offer. You end up with less than you should have gotten.

Thinking of it like buying a car. When you negotiate for a car, you know you can walk away and go to a different dealership if talks break down. That knowledge gives you leverage.

Injury claims don't work that way. There's no other insurance company to go to. If you're going to get any money, it's coming from the at-fault driver's liability coverage, your own UM/UIM coverage, or some combination. You're stuck with these parties.

Understand the dynamic you're in, not the one you're used to from other contexts.

It's a Process

The most important thing to understand about settlement negotiation is that it's a process.

The first offer tells you basically nothing. It's a starting position, not a serious assessment of your case's value. After several rounds of back and forth, a clearer picture emerges of how the other side is actually valuing the case and what compromise might be possible.

It's also important to try to understand why the insurance company is doing what they're doing.

Their evaluation process is opaque. It's subject to pressures and incentives that may have nothing to do with your specific case—things like quarterly targets, adjuster caseloads, or corporate policies about certain types of claims. But it's not irrational.

When the insurance company takes a position that seems unfair or unreasonable, they may be responding to a perceived or actual weakness in your case. Maybe there's a gap in your treatment history. Maybe liability isn't as clear as you think. Maybe something in your medical records raised a red flag.

You want to understand what's driving their position so you can either address it head-on or adjust your own expectations accordingly.

Throughout the process, keep the statute of limitations in mind. In New Mexico, most car accident claims must be filed within three years of the accident. Negotiations can stretch on, but if you haven't filed a lawsuit before that deadline passes, you lose your leverage entirely — and your claim with it. Your attorney should be tracking this, but you should know about it too.

Why Big Numbers on Billboards Mean Nothing

Now that you understand how many factors influence settlement outcomes, let's revisit something we touched on earlier when discussing how to find the right attorney.

You've seen the advertisements. "$5 Million Verdict." "Millions Recovered for Our Clients." Big numbers on billboards, in television commercials, on bus benches.

It should now be apparent how meaningless those numbers are without more context.

An attorney got a $1 million result. Was that a $2 million case they bungled, or a $500,000 case they worked into an extraordinary result? The billboard doesn't tell you. It can't tell you, because the number alone reveals nothing.

The actual process that led to any given result is a combination of many factors: the facts of the case, the severity of the injuries, the insurance available, the personalities involved, how thoroughly the case was worked up, the pressures of litigation, the decisions made by the client, and often a fair amount of luck regarding which judge or jury ended up deciding the matter.

None of that appears on a billboard.

An attorney advertising a big verdict number is essentially telling you they believe you can be manipulated by big numbers. That's the message. Not "I'm a skilled negotiator." Not "I understand insurance coverage." Not "I'll treat you with respect and fight for a fair outcome." Just: "Here's a big number. Be impressed."

Don't be impressed. Ask the questions we discussed earlier. Find out how the attorney actually approaches cases, how they communicate, and whether they have experience with situations like yours. Those things matter. The billboard number doesn't.

Key Takeaways

- Pre-litigation negotiation involves adjusters using algorithms and databases to value cases. It's impersonal and doesn't capture qualitative factors.
- Filing a lawsuit is the main leverage when pre-litigation talks stall. Lawsuit does not equal trial—there are many opportunities to settle after filing.
- Litigation changes the dynamic: local defense attorneys, accruing defense costs, access to discovery, and potentially court-ordered mediation.
- Mediation uses a neutral facilitator to speed up negotiation. Offers happen in hours instead of weeks.
- Evaluate offers based on fairness compared to similar cases, not just the raw number.
- Middle-ground offers are hard because you simultaneously wonder if you can do better and fear you can do worse. That conflict often signals true compromise territory.
- Settlement decisions involve your goals and risk tolerance, not just case value.
- Negotiations can restart at almost any point, even during trial or appeal.
- Don't rush to your bottom line—you'll end up negotiating against yourself.
- This isn't like buying a car. You can't walk away to a competitor. You're stuck with these parties.
- The first offer tells you nothing. After several rounds, the picture clarifies. Try to understand what's driving the other side's position.

- Be skeptical of attorneys advertising big verdict numbers. Without context, those numbers are meaningless—and advertising them suggests the attorney thinks you can be manipulated by them.

CHAPTER 13

WHEN YOUR CASE GOES TO COURT

This chapter provides a high-level overview of the litigation process. It's meant to prepare you for discussions with your attorney, not to serve as a comprehensive guide.

Litigation involves many ins and outs that go beyond what any single chapter can cover—special rules about handling medical records, ways that case costs can increase or be shifted between parties, details about witness presentation, procedures for handling subpoenas, and much more. Your attorney should go in-depth on the things that matter for your specific case.

Sometimes a lawsuit gets filed because the statute of limitations is approaching. In New Mexico, most car accident injury claims must be filed within three years. If negotiations are still ongoing as that deadline nears, your attorney will file suit to preserve the claim — even if both sides expect to keep negotiating toward a settlement.

What follows is a preview of what to expect if your case moves from negotiation into the court system.

Litigation Does Not Mean Trial

The most important thing to understand: filing a lawsuit does not mean you're going to trial.

Litigation means filing a lawsuit and getting a case opened in the court system. That starts a process that could lead to trial—but most cases don't get there. The overwhelming majority settle somewhere along the way.

It's best to think of litigation as the next stage in the negotiation process. Filing suit increases pressure on the insurance company. It creates costs for them. It moves toward a resolution with a deadline attached. But it doesn't commit you to seeing the case through to a jury verdict.

Settlement can occur at any time during litigation—even during trial itself.

The Stages of Litigation

Once a lawsuit is filed, the case moves through several stages.

Discovery. Discovery is the formal process through which the parties to a case are required to make certain information available to each other. This typically happens in three ways.

Written discovery requests, officially called interrogatories, require you to answer questions in writing and under oath. The other side will ask about the accident, your injuries, your treatment, your work history, and other relevant topics. Your attorney will help you prepare your responses.

Document sharing, officially called requests for production, requires you to provide documentation. This might include medical records, employment records, photographs, or other materials relevant to your case.

Depositions are formal questioning sessions. Parties and witnesses may be required to answer questions while a court reporter creates a transcript. Depositions can also be video recorded. Your attorney will prepare you before your deposition and be present during it.

In some cases, physical examinations may be required. When someone claims injuries, they typically support those claims through testimony from their own medical experts. The other side may request that their expert witnesses be allowed to conduct an independent medical examination of the claimant. If this happens in your case, your attorney will explain what to expect.

Mediation. During or after discovery, the court will typically order the parties to participate in mediation. We discussed mediation in the previous chapter—a settlement conference with a neutral facilitator trying to help both sides reach agreement.

Trial. At some point, typically at the parties' request, the judge will schedule a trial date. If the case doesn't settle before then, the trial happens and a judge or jury makes a decision.

A great deal of preparation goes into trial—witness lists, exhibit preparation, jury selection, opening statements, examination of witnesses, closing arguments. The details are beyond the scope of this book. Your attorney will work with you extensively to prepare if your case reaches this stage.

Appeal. After trial, the side that loses has the opportunity to appeal. This means asking the New Mexico Court of Appeals to review the legal decisions made by the trial judge to determine whether they were in accordance with New Mexico law.

If the appeals court finds an error, they may return the case to the trial court for a new trial. If they find no error, they "affirm" the judgment—upholding the trial court's decision and ordering it to be enforced.

Each of these stages could fill a book of its own. What matters for now is understanding the general sequence and knowing that your attorney will guide you through the specifics.

How Long Does Litigation Take?

A typical injury case in New Mexico may go to trial somewhere between one and three years after the filing of the lawsuit. This is measured from when the lawsuit is filed, not from the date of the accident.

If there's an appeal after trial, add several more years.

These timelines vary based on the complexity of the case, the court's schedule, and how aggressively both sides pursue or delay proceedings. Your attorney can give you a better estimate based on the specifics of your situation and which court your case is in.

Remember: settlement can happen at any point along this timeline, and most cases do settle before trial.

A Note on Bernalillo County

In Bernalillo County, certain claims—generally those where the claimant is seeking less than $50,000—must participate in mandatory arbitration. This is a court-ordered process that functions differently from a traditional trial.

If your case is filed in Bernalillo County and this applies to you, your attorney will explain what mandatory arbitration means and how it relates to the other stages of litigation.

What Litigation Feels Like for Clients

For clients, litigation is mostly waiting.

The case trudges forward through procedural stages, most of which happen without your direct involvement. Attorneys file motions. Documents get exchanged. Deadlines come and go. You might not hear much for weeks at a time.

That waiting is punctuated by a few occasions where you personally have to be involved—usually in stressful ways. The main client involvement points are:

- Answering written discovery. You'll need to respond to interrogatories and help gather documents.
- Sitting for a deposition. You'll be questioned under oath by the other side's attorney while a court reporter transcribes everything.
- Participating in mediation. You'll attend the settlement conference, either in person or virtually, and be involved in decisions about offers and counteroffers.
- Testifying at trial. If your case goes that far, you'll tell your story to the judge or jury.

Depositions Are Often the Most Stressful

Clients who have gone through all these stages often tell me that sitting for a deposition was the most stressful part.

That might seem counterintuitive. You'd think trial would be the hardest—the stakes are highest, the courtroom is formal, there's a jury watching. But for many clients, trial brings a sense of relief. It's finally their chance to tell their story in open court. It's the "day in court" they've been waiting for.

A deposition is different. You're being questioned by the opposing attorney, whose job is to find weaknesses in your case. There's no jury to appeal to. It can feel like an interrogation.

Your attorney will work with you closely to prepare for your deposition. They'll explain what to expect, go over likely questions, and help you understand how to respond. You won't go in blind.

The same applies if you're required to undergo a physical examination by the other side's medical expert. Your attorney will prepare you for what that involves.

If You Lose at Trial

Going to trial means accepting the possibility of losing. If the jury doesn't rule in your favor, there can be significant consequences.

You'll likely still have to reimburse your attorney for case costs—the expenses that were advanced during litigation. Depending on the circumstances, you might also be liable for some of the other party's costs.

Before you decide to reject a settlement offer and proceed to trial, have a realistic discussion with your attorney about these possibilities. Understand what you're risking, not just what you might gain.

Appeals Are Uphill Battles

If you lose at trial, you have the right to appeal. But it's important to understand that most appeals are unsuccessful. The losing side faces an uphill battle.

The reason is that trial courts—as the courts presiding over the actual trial, hearing live testimony, and observing witnesses—are given substantial deference on many legal issues. The appeals court isn't going to second-guess every decision the trial judge made. They're looking for significant legal errors, and those don't occur in most cases.

Something else that surprises people: appeals don't involve new testimony or new evidence. The appeals court reviews the record that was created at the trial court level—the filings, documents, evidence, and transcripts. You don't get to present your case again. You're arguing that legal mistakes were made the first time.

The Biggest Misconception

The biggest misconception about litigation is that filing a lawsuit definitely means going to trial and getting a decision from a judge or jury.

It doesn't. Filing a lawsuit starts a lengthy process that could end in trial, but most cases settle along the way. The filing itself, the discovery process, the approach of a trial date—all of these create pressure that often leads to resolution.

Think of litigation as another stage in negotiation, one with higher stakes and greater pressure on both sides. The possibility of trial focuses everyone's attention. But the goal, in most cases, remains finding a fair settlement.

Key Takeaways

- This chapter is a high-level overview. Litigation involves many details your attorney will explain based on your specific case.
- Litigation does not mean trial. It starts a process that could lead to trial, but most cases settle.
- Stages include discovery (written questions, document sharing, depositions), mediation, trial, and potentially appeal.
- Typical timeline: one to three years from filing to trial. Appeals add years. Settlement can happen anytime.
- Client involvement points: answering discovery, sitting for deposition, participating in mediation, testifying at trial.
- Depositions are often the most stressful part for clients. Your attorney will prepare you.
- If you lose at trial, you may owe case costs and potentially some of the other side's costs. Understand the risks before rejecting settlement.
- Most appeals are unsuccessful. Appeals review the existing record—no new testimony or evidence.
- Think of litigation as the next stage of negotiation with increased pressure, not a commitment to trial.

CHAPTER 14

CLOSING YOUR CASE AND GETTING PAID

You've reached a settlement. The number has been agreed upon. Now you want your money.

People often think they can get a check the next day, or at least within a week. That's not how it works. Several things need to happen between agreeing on a settlement and actually receiving your take-home amount. Understanding the process helps you know what to expect—and why it takes longer than you might think.

The Settlement Agreement

When the sides agree on a number, that's not the end. It's the beginning of the documentation process.

The attorneys draw up a settlement agreement—a legally binding contract that spells out all the terms of the deal. This isn't just a piece of paper with a dollar figure on it. At a minimum, a settlement agreement makes crystal clear that the at-fault party and their insurance company are completely released from any further liability, that any pending litigation will be dismissed, and that the claimant will never seek more money from them.

That last point bears emphasis. Once you settle, you're done with that party. Forever. You cannot go back for more money, no matter what happens with your injuries down the road.

This is why timing matters. You need to be done with treatment, or have a clear understanding of what future treatment you'll need, or at least be making a deliberate decision with your eyes wide open. Settling too early—before you know the full extent of your injuries—can leave you with expenses that will never be covered.

It may take weeks for the attorneys to work out the details of the settlement agreement. Drafts get passed back and forth. Language gets negotiated. Terms get clarified. This is normal, but it takes time.

Signing and Execution

Once the settlement agreement is finalized, you'll need to sign it. This will likely require a notary to notarize your signature.

Your attorney will then provide the executed—meaning signed—agreement to the other side. It's usually at that point when the insurance company sends the settlement check.

Subrogation and Lien Negotiation

While waiting for the check, your attorney should be working on another piece of the puzzle.

If your health insurance paid for accident-related treatment, they have a subrogation claim—a right to be repaid from your settlement.

If any medical providers filed liens against your case, those need to be resolved too.

Your attorney contacts these subrogated carriers and lienholders to negotiate reductions and get final numbers. As we discussed earlier in this book, these amounts are often negotiable. But the negotiation takes time, and the final numbers need to be known before your attorney can tell you exactly what your take-home amount will be.

The Trust Account and Clearing Period

When the settlement check arrives, your attorney doesn't hand it straight to you. The check gets deposited into the attorney's trust account—a special account used to hold client funds.

Then there's a waiting period. Usually seven to ten business days to ensure the check clears.

This might seem overly cautious, but there's good reason for it. A careful attorney will not start disbursing funds quickly after receiving an insurance check. If the check bounces and the attorney has already written checks against it, the result is insufficient funds in the trust account. That causes serious problems—for you, for the attorney, and for the attorney's other clients whose funds are also held in that account.

Waiting for the check to clear is standard practice and protects everyone.

Final Disbursement

Even once the check clears, your attorney can't cut you a check until everything else is resolved.

The subrogation claims need to be finalized. The lien amounts need to be confirmed. All the numbers need to be known so the math works out correctly.

Once everything is in place, you'll receive a disbursement statement. This document spells out exactly what's coming out of your settlement and what your final take-home amount will be.

The math looks like this:

Total settlement amount, minus attorney fees, minus taxes on those fees (gross receipts tax, as we discussed earlier), minus reimbursement of case costs your attorney advanced, minus required payments to subrogated carriers or lienholders, equals your final take-home amount.

What You'll Actually Take Home

Here's a reality that surprises some people: in a typical case, the injured claimant takes home somewhere between 35% and 50% of the total settlement amount.

That percentage varies based on the circumstances. If there were significant case costs—expert witnesses, extensive discovery, a long litigation—more comes out. If subrogation or lien claims were substantial, more comes out. If there are insurance coverage issues where the available limits are less than the true value of your damages, that can affect the percentage as well.

Every case is different. But going in with realistic expectations about take-home amounts helps avoid disappointment at the end.

Timeline: Agreement to Check in Hand

In most cases, clients can expect to receive their final take-home check somewhere between thirty and sixty days after a settlement is agreed upon.

That accounts for drafting and negotiating the settlement agreement, signing and execution, waiting for the insurance company to issue the check, depositing and clearing the check, finalizing subrogation and lien negotiations, and preparing the final disbursement.

Some cases move faster. Some take longer. But thirty to sixty days is a reasonable expectation for a typical case.

After a Verdict

If your case went to trial and you won a judgment in your favor, the collection process depends on what the other side decides to do.

If they accept the verdict and decide to pay, the process looks like a settlement. The money gets collected, deposited, cleared, and disbursed according to the same general framework.

If they want to keep fighting by filing an appeal, things get more complicated. They may be able to get a court order "staying execution" of the judgment. In plain terms, that means they don't have to pay the judgment while the appeal is pending.

The court may require them to post an appeal bond—money set aside to guarantee payment if the appeal fails. But the appeal process can take years, and you won't see your money until it's resolved.

What Can Cause Delays

Several things can delay the closing process beyond the typical timeline.

Defense inserting new terms. Sometimes the defense tries to insert previously unmentioned terms into the settlement agreement—conditions that weren't part of the original deal. This requires negotiation to resolve and can slow things down.

Cases involving children. If the injured person is a minor, the settlement may require court approval. This process, called minor settlement approval, adds steps and time. We'll discuss this in a later chapter.

Unresponsive subrogated carriers or lienholders. Your attorney needs final numbers from health insurers and lienholders before disbursing funds. If they're slow to respond or unwilling to negotiate, it creates delays.

Insurance company delays. Sometimes the insurance company simply takes longer than expected to issue the check. There may be no good explanation. It's frustrating, but it happens.

If your case is experiencing unusual delays, ask your attorney what's causing the holdup and what's being done to move things forward.

Multiple Defendants

If there's more than one party on the other side of your case, you might go through this process at different times with each defendant.

You could settle relatively quickly with one defendant while still fighting through litigation with another. A settlement with one party doesn't necessarily end the whole case.

This matters because you need to understand what any particular settlement means for your overall situation. Does settling with Defendant A resolve everything, or are you still pursuing claims against Defendant B? Will there be more money coming, or is this it?

Discuss this with your attorney before agreeing to any partial settlement. Make sure you understand whether the settlement ends the whole case or just part of it.

Key Takeaways

- Settlement doesn't mean immediate payment. Expect thirty to sixty days from agreement to check in hand.
- The settlement agreement is a binding contract that completely releases the other party. Once you sign, you can never go back for more.
- The check goes into a trust account and must clear (seven to ten business days) before funds can be disbursed.
- Final disbursement can't happen until subrogation and lien claims are resolved with confirmed amounts.
- Your disbursement statement shows everything that comes out: attorney fees, taxes, case costs, subrogation, and liens.
- Typical take-home is 35–50% of the total settlement, but every case is different.
- After a verdict, collection depends on whether the other side pays or appeals. Appeals can delay payment for years.
- Delays can result from defense adding new terms, minor settlement approval requirements, unresponsive lienholders, or insurance company slowness.

- With multiple defendants, you may settle with some while continuing to fight others. Understand whether a settlement ends the whole case.

PART 3

SPECIAL SITUATIONS

As if injury claims weren't complicated enough, certain situations add layers of complexity and present their own pitfalls.

This section covers claims involving Medicare recipients, cases where the injured person is a child, wrongful death claims, insurance bad faith, and structured settlements. Each of these topics could fill its own book. What follows is an overview to help you recognize when one of these situations applies and understand why working with a skilled attorney is essential when they do.

CHAPTER 15

MEDICARE AND YOUR INJURY CLAIM

If you're on Medicare, your injury claim involves additional rules and requirements that don't apply to people with private health insurance. These rules come from federal law, and the consequences for getting them wrong can be serious.

This chapter explains what Medicare recipients need to know and why working closely with your attorney on these issues is essential.

Why Medicare Is Different

When Medicare pays for medical treatment related to your accident, federal law says they have a right to be paid back.

This comes from the Medicare Secondary Payer Recovery Act. The principle is straightforward: if Medicare paid for your injuries and a different entity should have paid—like the at-fault driver's liability insurance—then Medicare can recover what they spent from any settlement or judgment you receive.

So far, this sounds similar to the subrogation claims we discussed earlier with private health insurance. In Medicare terminology, these payments are called Medicare conditional payments. And like other subrogation claims, conditional payment amounts can often be negotiated down.

But that's where the similarities end. Medicare has rules that go beyond what private insurers can do, and the stakes for non-compliance are much higher.

Consequence for Non-Compliance: Losing Eligibility

Here's the most serious difference. If Medicare's conditional payment claim is not properly resolved, you could lose your Medicare eligibility.

That's not a typo. Failing to address Medicare's recovery rights can result in losing your health coverage.

This is why it's imperative that Medicare conditional payments be addressed in every case involving a Medicare recipient. It's not optional. It's not something to deal with later. Your attorney needs to handle this, and you need to make sure it's happening.

Medicare Set-Asides: Protecting Future Treatment

Unlike private health insurers, Medicare's right to reimbursement doesn't necessarily end when your claim ends.

If your settlement involves the potential for future medical treatment related to your accident, Medicare's interests may need to be taken into account. This means that some portion of your settlement might need to be set aside to pay for future accident-related care before Medicare starts covering those expenses again.

This is called a Medicare set-aside.

The law in this area is not entirely clear. There are ongoing legal debates, and guidance from CMS—the Centers for Medicare and Medicaid Services—has been murky. But the requirement appears to exist, and ignoring it creates risk.

How much needs to be set aside? That depends on your specific situation—what future treatment you're likely to need, what it will cost, and actuarial calculations about timing and life expectancy.

This is not something you or your attorney should try to figure out on your own.

Using Expert Vendors for Set-Aside Analysis

There are companies that specialize in Medicare set-aside planning. They employ experts who analyze your treatment needs, review medical records, research costs, apply actuarial data, and produce a formal plan that calculates an appropriate set-aside amount in current dollars.

If your case needs a Medicare set-aside due to expected future treatment, one of these vendors should be engaged. This is specialized work that requires specialized expertise.

The cost of a set-aside analysis varies, and not every case justifies the expense. A small settlement might not warrant spending thousands of dollars on expert analysis. But for cases with significant future treatment needs, it's an essential step.

When Is a Set-Aside Necessary?

This is where things get frustrating. The official guidance on when a Medicare set-aside is required in liability cases is unclear.

Some attorneys believe, based on certain federal memos, that set-asides are never required in liability cases—only in workers' compensation cases. In my opinion, that interpretation is too risky. The potential consequences of getting this wrong are too serious to rely on an aggressive reading of ambiguous guidance.

My approach: it's best practice to recommend a set-aside analysis whenever there's a reasonable probability that you'll need future medical care related to your accident injuries. Better to address it deliberately than to discover years later that you should have.

What the Process Looks Like

Your attorney should contact Medicare early in your case to get information about conditional payments—what Medicare has paid so far for your accident-related treatment.

One important note: Medicare does not review or approve set-asides in liability cases. Unlike workers' compensation cases, where you can submit a set-aside proposal to CMS for approval, there's no such process for liability claims. You're making your best judgment based on expert analysis, not getting a government stamp of approval.

This is another reason why working with experienced vendors and attorneys matters. You're navigating uncertain territory, and you need people who understand the landscape.

What You Need to Provide

From your end, the most important thing is simple: give your attorney your Medicare ID and number at the outset of your case.

Your attorney should take it from there—contacting Medicare, tracking conditional payments, determining whether a set-aside analysis is appropriate, and engaging vendors if needed.

But it starts with you providing that basic information. If you're on Medicare, tell your attorney immediately and provide your Medicare card.

The Client's Decision

Ultimately, whether to pay for a Medicare set-aside analysis is your decision.

Not every recovery justifies the cost. If your settlement is modest and future treatment needs are minimal or speculative, spending several thousand dollars on a formal set-aside analysis might not make sense.

But the choice should be made deliberately, in discussion with your attorney. You need to understand the risks of not doing a set-aside, weigh them against the costs of doing one, and make an informed decision.

Don't let this issue slide by without consideration. Address it one way or another.

Medicare Eligibility Can Arise Mid-Case

Here's something that surprises people: Medicare issues can come up even if you weren't on Medicare at the time of your accident.

If you become eligible for Medicare while your case is pending, these rules start to apply. If you're going to become eligible in the next couple of years—because you're approaching age sixty-five or because of a disability determination—that can affect how your settlement needs to be structured.

This is another reason to keep your attorney informed about changes in your situation. If your Medicare status changes, or is about to change, your attorney needs to know.

Key Takeaways

- Medicare has special rules under federal law (Medicare Secondary Payer Recovery Act) that go beyond ordinary subrogation.
- Medicare conditional payments must be resolved, or you risk losing Medicare eligibility.
- If future treatment is expected, a Medicare set-aside may be required—money set aside from your settlement to cover future care before Medicare resumes paying.
- Set-aside analysis should be done by expert vendors, not by you or your attorney alone.
- Official guidance on when set-asides are required is unclear. Best practice: consider a set-aside analysis whenever future care is reasonably probable.
- Medicare does not review or approve set-asides in liability cases. You're relying on expert judgment in uncertain territory.
- Provide your Medicare ID and number to your attorney at the start of your case.
- Whether to pay for a set-aside analysis is your decision, but make it deliberately after discussing with your attorney.
- Medicare issues can arise even if you weren't on Medicare at the time of the accident—eligibility during or shortly after your case matters.

CHAPTER 16

CLAIMS INVOLVING CHILDREN

When the injured person is a child, special rules apply. Children lack the legal capacity to sign binding contracts—including settlement agreements. This creates additional requirements and protections that don't exist in adult claims.

If your child was injured in a car accident, or if you're a family member helping navigate a child's claim, this chapter explains what you need to know.

Why Children's Claims Are Different

An adult can review a settlement offer, decide it's fair, sign a release, and be bound by that decision. A child cannot.

The law recognizes that children lack the capacity to make these decisions for themselves. They can't fully understand the consequences of accepting a settlement. They can't evaluate whether an offer is fair. They can't protect their own interests the way an adult can.

Because of this, the legal system builds in protections to make sure children aren't taken advantage of—by insurance companies, by attorneys, or even by their own parents.

Court Approval Is Required

In a typical injury claim involving a child, a parent or guardian signs documents on the child's behalf. But that signature alone isn't enough to make a settlement binding.

For the settlement to be final and enforceable, it generally requires court approval.

The court's job is to protect the child. The judge reviews the settlement to make sure it's fair to the child—not structured in a way that benefits the parents or the attorney at the child's expense. The court also looks at how the settlement money will be handled to ensure it will be held and invested appropriately for the child's benefit, not used by parents for unrelated expenses.

This process adds time and steps to resolving a child's claim, but it exists for good reason.

The Guardian Ad Litem

To help with this review, the court will typically appoint a guardian ad litem.

A guardian ad litem is an independent person—often an attorney—appointed to investigate the circumstances of the settlement and represent the child's interests in the court proceeding. They're not the family's attorney. They're not the insurance company's representative. They work for the court.

The guardian ad litem reviews the case, examines the proposed settlement, and makes a report and recommendation to the judge. They might interview family members, review medical records, and assess whether the settlement amount is reasonable given the child's injuries.

The judge considers this recommendation when deciding whether to approve the settlement.

Conflicts of Interest

Here's a complication that arises in some family accident cases: conflicts of interest.

Let's say there's a car accident where both drivers share some fault. Any passengers in either vehicle are without fault—they weren't driving, so they bear no responsibility for the collision.

Now imagine a situation where a parent was driving and children were passengers. All of them were injured. If there's any potential that the parent's driving contributed to the accident—and therefore to the children's injuries—a conflict of interest exists.

An adult passenger in that situation could acknowledge the conflict and choose to waive it, allowing the same attorney to represent both the driver and the passenger. Adults have the capacity to make that informed decision.

Children do not.

Because children can't make informed decisions about waiving conflicts of interest, they may need separate legal representation. If dad was driving and the kids were passengers, and there's any argument that dad's driving contributed to the crash, the same attorney cannot represent the whole family. The children need their own lawyer—someone whose only duty is to protect their interests.

This can feel awkward or even offensive to parents who would never do anything against their children's interests. But the rule exists precisely because children can't protect themselves. The legal system doesn't assume bad intentions. It simply requires structural protections.

How the Settlement Money Is Handled

Once a child's settlement is approved, the court also oversees how the money is managed.

The goal is to make sure the funds are protected and available for the child's benefit—not spent by parents on unrelated expenses before the child reaches adulthood.

There's no one-size-fits-all approach. The court has flexibility to approve arrangements that make sense for the specific situation. Options might include structured settlements that pay out over time, accounts established under the Uniform Transfers to Minors Act, or other vehicles designed to protect the funds.

The judge considers the size of the settlement, the child's age, any ongoing needs related to the injury, and the costs associated with different options. The focus is always on what best protects the child.

The Bottom Line

The number one takeaway for claims involving children is this: everyone involved should be looking out for the child's best interests.

The attorney should focus on getting a fair result for the child. The parents should be advocating for their child's needs. The guardian ad litem should be providing independent oversight. The judge should be scrutinizing the settlement to make sure it's appropriate.

All of these layers exist because children legally lack the capacity to protect themselves. They can't evaluate whether a settlement is fair. They can't manage a large sum of money. They can't identify conflicts of interest.

The system is designed to surround them with people who can.

If your child has been injured, make sure you're working with an attorney who understands these requirements and prioritizes your child's interests above all else.

Key Takeaways

- Children lack legal capacity to sign binding contracts, so special rules apply to their injury claims.
- Settlement of a child's claim generally requires court approval to ensure it's fair and the money will be properly managed.
- The court typically appoints a guardian ad litem to investigate and make recommendations about the settlement.
- Children cannot waive conflicts of interest. If a family member's fault contributed to the child's injuries, the child needs separate legal representation.
- Settlement funds are managed through court-approved arrangements designed to protect the money for the child's benefit.
- Everyone involved—attorney, parents, guardian ad litem, judge—should focus on protecting the child's best interests.

CHAPTER 17
WRONGFUL DEATH CASES

When someone dies as a result of a car accident, the legal claim that follows is different from a personal injury claim. New Mexico's Wrongful Death Act establishes specific procedures for who can bring a claim, how the case proceeds, and how any recovery is distributed.

If you've lost a family member in an accident, this chapter explains what you need to know about wrongful death claims in New Mexico.

The Purpose of the Wrongful Death Act

The Wrongful Death Act seeks to create clear rules. When someone dies, multiple family members may have an interest in pursuing a legal claim. Without structure, this could lead to disputes—competing claims, disagreements about settlement, arguments over who gets what.

The WDA prevents this by establishing a single path forward. It designates who can bring the claim and sets out exactly how any recovery must be distributed. The rules are fixed by law, not left to negotiation among grieving family members.

The Personal Representative

A wrongful death claim in New Mexico must be brought by a personal representative (PR) of the wrongful death estate.

This is an important distinction. If you've dealt with probate before, you may be familiar with the concept of a personal representative handling a deceased person's estate. But a probate personal representative is not automatically a wrongful death personal representative. These are separate appointments.

You don't need to open a probate proceeding to bring a wrongful death claim. But you do need a wrongful death PR appointment.

How the Appointment Works

Here's how the process typically unfolds.

A family member of the deceased contacts an attorney. The attorney files a petition with the court requesting appointment of a personal representative for the wrongful death estate.

Who can serve as PR? Generally, anyone. It's often a family member, but it can also be another person—sometimes an attorney. The specific individual matters less than the role they'll play.

Once appointed, the PR has legal duties to make sure any recovery is distributed in accordance with the Wrongful Death Act. A family member serving as PR doesn't get an advantage or a larger share than other family members. The PR is a fiduciary, acting on behalf of everyone entitled to recovery under the law.

How the Claim Proceeds

The personal representative is empowered to bring the wrongful death claim on behalf of the estate.

The PR typically enters into a fee agreement with an attorney to investigate and litigate the claim. If a lawsuit is filed, the PR is named as the plaintiff—not individual family members.

From there, the mechanics of litigation are similar to other injury cases. There's discovery, potentially mediation, and either settlement or trial. The difference is that the PR, not the deceased or surviving family members, is the legal party pursuing the claim.

Loss of Consortium Claims

Family members may also have their own loss of consortium claims—compensation for the damage to their relationship with the deceased.

These claims are legally separate from the wrongful death claim itself. A spouse, for example, might have a loss of consortium claim for the loss of their partner's companionship and support.

Your attorney can explain whether loss of consortium claims apply in your situation and how they relate to the wrongful death case.

How Recovery Is Distributed

If there's a recovery—whether through settlement or verdict—the Wrongful Death Act sets out exactly how the money must be distributed.

The distribution depends on the deceased's family situation. The rules differ based on whether the deceased had a spouse, had children, had surviving parents, or had siblings. The Act specifies who receives what share under each scenario.

Importantly, this distribution is not determined by the deceased's will. Whatever the deceased may have intended for their estate, the wrongful death recovery follows the statutory formula. The PR has no discretion to alter these distributions. They're required by law.

This can sometimes surprise families. But the fixed distribution rules prevent disputes and ensure fair treatment of all beneficiaries.

Damages in Wrongful Death Cases

The damages available in a wrongful death case include everything the injured person could have recovered if they had survived—medical expenses incurred before death, pain and suffering experienced before death, lost income, and so on.

Beyond that, wrongful death claims include compensation for the value of life itself.

This is a subjective and profound concept. What is a human life worth? There's no formula. New Mexico juries have awarded everything from hundreds of thousands of dollars to tens of millions for this component of damages, depending on the circumstances and the life that was lost.

The value of life is separate from economic losses. It attempts to compensate for the loss of the person—their presence, their relationships, their future.

The PR's Authority Over Settlement

Here's something important for family members to understand: the personal representative—and only the personal representative—has the power to agree to a settlement figure.

Other family members cannot override that decision. If the PR decides to accept a settlement offer, that's the decision. If the PR decides to reject an offer and continue litigating, that's also the decision.

This can create tension, especially in families where opinions differ about what's fair or how to proceed. But the structure exists for a reason. Someone has to have final authority, and the law places that authority with the PR.

If you're a family member with concerns about how a wrongful death case is being handled, you can raise those concerns with the PR or the attorney. But understand that the PR holds the decision-making power.

Working with an Attorney

Wrongful death cases are emotionally difficult and legally complex. The PR appointment process, the claim itself, the distribution rules, and the damages calculations all require careful attention.

If you've lost a family member in an accident, work with an attorney who has experience handling wrongful death claims in New Mexico. They can guide you through the PR appointment, explain your rights and options, and help ensure that the claim is handled properly.

Key Takeaways

- New Mexico's Wrongful Death Act establishes who can bring a claim and how recovery is distributed.
- A wrongful death claim must be brought by a personal representative of the wrongful death estate—separate from any probate PR.
- The PR is appointed by the court, can be a family member or another person, and has legal duties to follow the WDA.
- Distribution of any recovery is set by law based on family situation—not by the deceased's will. The PR cannot alter these distributions.
- Damages include everything the deceased could have recovered, plus compensation for the value of life itself—a subjective amount that varies widely.
- Only the PR has authority to agree to a settlement. Family members cannot override that decision.
- Loss of consortium claims are separate from the wrongful death claim itself.
- Work with an attorney experienced in New Mexico wrongful death cases.

CHAPTER 18

INSURANCE BAD FAITH

Insurance companies have legal duties about how they handle claims. When they fail to meet those duties, it's called bad faith—and it can give rise to additional legal claims beyond the underlying injury case.

This chapter explains what bad faith means, when it applies, and what you can do about it.

The Legal Framework

New Mexico law imposes obligations on insurance companies through multiple sources. Common law—judge-made law developed through court decisions over time—establishes certain duties. Statutory law—rules enacted by the legislature—adds more. Regulations from the Office of the Superintendent of Insurance provide additional requirements.

There are many nuances to these rules, including differences for various policies and different claims. But they all boil down to one overarching principle: insurance companies must treat their insureds fairly.

When an insurance company violates this principle, a bad faith claim may be available.

Common Bad Faith Behaviors

A variety of behaviors can technically violate these rules. But the most common—and the easiest to identify—fall into three categories.

Improper delay. The insurance company drags its feet, failing to process claims or make payments within reasonable timeframes. They may request unnecessary documentation, fail to respond to communications, or simply let claims sit without action.

Improper denial. The insurance company denies coverage or denies a claim when the denial isn't justified under the policy terms or the law. They may misinterpret policy language, apply exclusions that don't actually apply, or refuse to pay for reasons that don't hold up.

Intentional undervaluation. The insurance company acknowledges the claim but deliberately undervalues it, offering far less than what the claim is actually worth. They may ignore evidence, rely on biased evaluations, or simply lowball in hopes that the claimant will accept less than they're owed.

These behaviors aren't just frustrating. When they violate the duties the insurance company owes, they can form the basis of a bad faith claim.

Which Insurance Company Is Liable for Bad Faith?

There's a critical distinction between bad faith by the at-fault driver's insurance company and bad faith by your own insurance company.

It starts with this: the policy of insurance is a contract. The at-fault driver's insurance company has a contract with the at-fault driver—their insured. They don't have a contract with you.

Your own insurance company, on the other hand, does have a contract with you. You're their insured. They owe you the duties that come with that relationship.

Because bad faith is essentially a breach of duty, bad faith claims generally arise where those duties exist—between a company and the person insured by that company.

This means bad faith claims most commonly involve your own insurance company. When your UM/UIM carrier delays, denies, or undervalues your claim, they may be breaching duties they owe directly to you.

What about the at-fault driver's insurance company? In theory, New Mexico law does permit some claims by an injured party against the at-fault driver's insurer. But the courts have imposed significant hurdles to these claims. They're harder to bring and harder to win.

A Note on Same-Company Situations

Sometimes you and the at-fault driver have the same insurance company. Does that change things?

Not as much as you might think. Even if the same company issued both policies, each policy is a separate contract. The company's duties to you flow from your policy. Their duties to the at-fault driver flow from that driver's policy.

Importantly, there should be different adjusters working each claim. If the same adjuster is handling both—your claim against the at-fault driver's liability coverage and the at-fault driver's interests—that could itself be evidence of bad faith. The potential for conflict of interest is obvious.

Remedies for Bad Faith

What can you recover if bad faith is established?

At a baseline, you want to recover the coverage amount that should have been paid. If the insurance company improperly denied or undervalued your claim, you're entitled to what you should have received in the first place.

Beyond that, bad faith cases often bring an opportunity for fee-shifting. This means you may be able to get the insurance company to pay your attorney's fees. In ordinary injury cases, attorney fees come out of your recovery. In bad faith cases, the company that acted in bad faith may have to pay them separately. This is often a significant advantage.

Additional damages may be available depending on the nature of the bad faith and what harm it caused. If the company's conduct was particularly egregious, punitive damages might come into play.

How Bad Faith Claims Work

A bad faith claim can be brought as a separate lawsuit, or it can be added to your existing injury case. There are strategic and timing considerations to discuss with your attorney.

Typically, it's preferable to bring everything together in one case. This minimizes costs and timelines. It enables a potential global resolution where everything gets settled at once. It also prevents arguments by any party that they were deprived of the opportunity to weigh in on particular issues.

But sometimes there are reasons to handle things separately—for example, if the bad faith becomes apparent only after the injury case has progressed. Your attorney can advise on the best approach for your situation.

What to Do If You Suspect Bad Faith

If you think your insurance company is acting in bad faith, start with the policy document itself.

The first question I ask in a consultation about potential bad faith is whether the prospective client has a copy of their policy. Everything flows from there.

We need to see what the insurance company promised to do. Then we evaluate whether that promise complies with New Mexico law—sometimes policy language itself is problematic. Then we evaluate whether the company actually did what they were supposed to do under the policy and the law.

If you don't have your policy, request a copy from your insurance company. You're entitled to it.

Document everything. Keep records of communications, delays, and denials. Note dates and times. Save emails and letters. If you have phone conversations, follow up with an email summarizing what was discussed.

Then talk to an attorney who handles insurance bad faith claims. They can evaluate whether what you're experiencing crosses the line from aggressive claims handling to actionable bad faith.

Key Takeaways

- New Mexico law requires insurance companies to treat their insureds fairly. Violations can give rise to bad faith claims.
- Common bad faith behaviors include improper delay, improper denial, and intentional undervaluation.
- Bad faith claims typically involve your own insurance company, because that's where the contractual duties exist. Claims against the at-fault driver's insurer face significant legal hurdles.
- Even if you and the at-fault driver have the same insurance company, each policy is a separate contract with separate duties. The same adjuster should not handle both sides.
- Remedies for bad faith include the coverage that should have been paid, potential fee-shifting (company pays your attorney fees), and possibly additional damages.
- Bad faith claims can be brought separately or combined with your injury case. Discuss strategy with your attorney.
- If you suspect bad faith, start with your policy document. Document everything. Talk to an attorney who handles these claims.

CONCLUSION

This book was never meant to make you a lawyer. It wasn't meant to convince you to handle everything yourself. The legal system is complex, insurance companies are sophisticated, and the stakes are too high for most people to go it alone.

What this book was meant to do is show you that you can understand this process — and that you deserve to.

You're not a passive recipient of whatever your attorney and the insurance company work out between themselves. You're a person with a stake in the outcome, capable of understanding the decisions that shape your case. You can learn how insurance coverage works. You can grasp how cases are valued. You can follow the logic of settlement negotiations and understand what happens if your case goes to court.

None of that requires a law degree. It requires someone willing to explain things clearly — and a reader willing to engage.

You've done your part. You've taken the time to learn a process that most people face blind. That puts you ahead of nearly everyone who goes through this.

Now put it to use.

Work with your attorney as a partner, not a passenger. Ask questions when something doesn't make sense. Push back when you're uncertain. Expect clear answers and regular communication. Understand that your attorney brings expertise and experience you don't have — but also understand that it's your case, your injuries, your life.

The best outcomes come when informed clients work with skilled attorneys toward a resolution that's fair and makes sense. That's the relationship this book was designed to support.

You're ready for it.

APPENDIX A
GLOSSARY OF TERMS

Actual Cash Value (ACV). The fair market value of a vehicle immediately before an accident. Used to determine whether a vehicle is a total loss and how much the insurance company will pay for it.

Appeal. A request to a higher court (in New Mexico, the Court of Appeals) to review legal decisions made by the trial court. Appeals review the existing record—no new testimony or evidence is presented.

Appeal Bond. Money the losing party may be required to set aside to guarantee payment if their appeal fails. Allows them to delay payment of a judgment while the appeal is pending.

Bad Faith. When an insurance company fails to meet its legal duties to treat its insureds fairly. Common examples include improper delay, improper denial, and intentional undervaluation of claims.

Bodily Injury. Physical harm to a person rather than property damage. Bodily injury claims seek compensation for medical expenses, pain and suffering, lost wages, and related losses.

Collision Coverage. Insurance coverage on your own policy that pays for repairs to your vehicle regardless of who was at fault in the accident.

Comparative Negligence. New Mexico's rule that reduces a claimant's recovery in proportion to their share of fault. If you're found 10% at fault, your recovery is reduced by 10%.

Complaint. The legal document that initiates a lawsuit. Filing a complaint causes the court to open an official case record with a case number.

Compensatory Damages. Money awarded to compensate an injured person for their losses. Includes medical expenses, lost wages, pain and suffering, loss of enjoyment of life, and similar categories.

Comprehensive Coverage. Insurance coverage on your own policy that pays for damage to your vehicle from causes other than collision, such as theft, vandalism, or weather.

Conditional Payments. Medicare's term for payments made for treatment related to an accident. Medicare has a right to recover these payments from any settlement or judgment.

Contingency Fee. A fee arrangement where the attorney's payment is a percentage of the recovery. If there's no recovery, there's no fee.

Costs. Expenses paid to others to move a case forward—copying charges for records, filing fees, court reporter fees, expert witness fees. Distinct from attorney fees.

Declarations Page. The section of an insurance policy that summarizes your specific coverages, limits, and premiums. Sometimes called the "dec page."

Defendant. The party being sued in a lawsuit. In a car accident case, typically the at-fault driver and sometimes their insurance company.

Demand. A formal request for compensation, typically presented in a demand letter or demand package that outlines the facts of the case, the injuries, and the amount sought.

Demand Package. A demand accompanied by supporting materials such as police reports, medical records, and medical bills.

Deposition. Formal questioning of a party or witness under oath, outside of court, with a court reporter transcribing the testimony. May be video recorded.

Diminished Value. The reduction in a vehicle's market value after it has been in an accident and repaired. A car with collision history is worth less than one without.

Discovery. The formal process in litigation through which parties exchange information. Includes written questions (interrogatories), document requests, and depositions.

Disbursement Statement. A document showing how settlement funds are distributed—total recovery minus attorney fees, taxes, costs, subrogation, and liens equals the client's take-home amount.

Exclusion. A provision in an insurance policy that specifies situations or circumstances not covered by the policy.

Expert Witness. A person with specialized knowledge—such as a doctor, accident reconstructionist, or economist—who provides testimony to help the judge or jury understand technical aspects of a case.

Fault. Responsibility for causing an accident. In New Mexico, fault determines which party's insurance pays and can be divided between multiple parties under comparative negligence rules.

Fee-Shifting. When one party has to pay the other party's attorney fees. Available in some bad faith and statutory claims.

First-Party Claim. A claim made against your own insurance policy, such as a UM/UIM claim or a claim under your collision coverage.

Gross Receipts Tax (GRT). A New Mexico tax on business receipts. Attorneys must pay GRT on their fees, which is typically passed on to the client. Rates vary by location.

Guardian Ad Litem. A person appointed by the court to represent the interests of a child in legal proceedings, such as evaluating whether a proposed settlement is fair.

Interrogatories. Written questions that must be answered in writing and under oath as part of the discovery process.

Judgment. The official decision of a court at the end of a trial.

Letter of Protection. A letter from an attorney to a medical provider promising to pay for treatment from the client's eventual settlement. Allows treatment when the patient can't pay upfront.

Liability Coverage. Insurance that pays for bodily injury and property damage that the policyholder causes to others. Required by New Mexico law for all registered vehicles.

Lien. A legal claim against a settlement. Medical providers may file liens to ensure they get paid from the recovery for treatment they provided.

Loss of Consortium. Damages claimed by a spouse or family member for harm to their relationship with the injured person—loss of companionship, support, and similar impacts.

Loss of Enjoyment of Life. Damages for the activities, hobbies, and pleasures the injured person can no longer participate in because of their injuries.

Loss of Use. Compensation for time without access to your vehicle while it's being repaired or replaced.

Med Pay (Medical Payments Coverage). Coverage on your auto policy that pays medical bills up to a specified limit, regardless of who was at fault.

Mediation. A settlement process where a neutral third party (mediator) helps both sides try to reach an agreement. Often ordered by the court during litigation.

Medicare Set-Aside. Money from a settlement set aside to pay for future accident-related medical treatment before Medicare resumes paying. May be required when the claimant is on Medicare.

Minor Settlement Approval. Court approval required for settlements involving children, to ensure the settlement is fair and the funds will be properly managed.

Negligence. The failure to use reasonable care, resulting in harm to another person. The legal basis for most car accident injury claims.

Offset. In UIM claims, the subtraction of the at-fault driver's liability limits from your UIM limits. If they have $25,000 liability and you have $50,000 UIM, the offset means your effective UIM coverage is $25,000.

Pain and Suffering. Compensation for the physical pain and emotional distress caused by injuries.

Per Accident Limit. The maximum amount an insurance policy will pay for all claims arising from a single accident, no matter how many people are injured.

Per Person Limit. The maximum amount an insurance policy will pay for any one person's injuries in an accident.

Personal Representative (PR). In wrongful death cases, the person appointed by the court to bring the claim on behalf of the estate. Has legal duties to distribute any recovery according to the Wrongful Death Act.

Plaintiff. The party who files a lawsuit. In a car accident case, typically the injured person or, in wrongful death cases, the personal representative.

Policy Limits. The maximum amount an insurance policy will pay. Often expressed as two numbers (per person/per accident), such as $25,000/$50,000.

Property Damage. Damage to physical property, such as vehicles rather than bodily injury. Property damage claims are typically handled separately from injury claims.

Punitive Damages. Damages meant to punish the at-fault party for particularly bad conduct, such as drunk driving. Not meant to compensate the injured person but to deter similar behavior.

Release. A legal document signed when settling a claim that gives up all future rights to seek additional compensation from the released party. Final and binding.

Requests for Production. Formal requests during discovery for the other party to provide documents and other materials relevant to the case.

Recovery. The money obtained through settlement or verdict in an injury claim. Used interchangeably with "settlement" or "judgment amount."

Salvage Vehicle. In New Mexico, a vehicle that has been declared a total loss. Cannot be registered for public roads until proof of repair is provided to MVD.

Settlement. An agreement between the parties to resolve a claim without trial. The injured party receives compensation in exchange for releasing all claims.

Settlement Agreement. The legally binding contract that documents a settlement. Spells out all terms, including the amount paid, the release of liability, and dismissal of any pending litigation.

Stacking. Combining UM/UIM coverage from multiple vehicles or policies to increase the total available coverage. New Mexico allows stacking in certain circumstances.

Stay of Execution. A court order that delays enforcement of a judgment, typically while an appeal is pending.

Statute of Limitations. The deadline for filing a lawsuit. Miss it and you lose your right to pursue the claim, regardless of how strong your case is. The deadline varies depending on the type of claim involved — discuss the applicable deadlines with your attorney early in your case.

Subrogation. The right of an insurance company that paid for your treatment to be reimbursed from your settlement. If your health insurer paid accident-related bills, they may recover that money from your recovery.

Third-Party Claim. A claim made against someone else's insurance policy, such as a claim against the at-fault driver's liability coverage.

Total Loss. When a vehicle's repair cost plus salvage value exceeds its pre-accident actual cash value. The insurance company pays the ACV rather than repairing the vehicle.

Trial Court. The court where a case is first heard, evidence is presented, and witnesses testify. In New Mexico, this is typically the district court. Decisions of the trial court can be appealed to the Court of Appeals.

Trust Account. A special bank account where attorneys hold client funds, such as settlement proceeds, separate from the firm's operating funds.

UM/UIM (Uninsured/Underinsured Motorist Coverage). Coverage on your own policy that protects you when the at-fault driver has no insurance (UM), not enough insurance (UIM), or was never identified (hit-and-run).

Umbrella Policy. An additional liability insurance policy that provides coverage beyond the limits of a standard auto or homeowner's policy. Few individuals carry umbrella coverage.

UTMA (Uniform Transfers to Minors Act). A law that provides a way to manage money for minors. UTMA accounts are sometimes used to hold settlement funds for children.

Verdict. The decision of a jury (or judge in a bench trial) at the end of a trial.

Wrongful Death Act. New Mexico law that establishes who can bring a claim when someone dies due to another's negligence, and how any recovery must be distributed among family members.

APPENDIX B
WHAT TO DO IMMEDIATELY AFTER AN ACCIDENT

This book assumes you're already navigating the claims process. But if you're reading this right after an accident — or want guidance to share with someone else — here are the five most important things to do.

1. Get to safety.

This is paramount. Get yourself and any passengers away from the road. If your vehicle is operable, move it out of traffic. If the other driver is hostile or confrontational, do not escalate. Remove yourself to a safe location and contact law enforcement from there.

2. Get required medical care.

If you need to be transported to an emergency room, do it. Don't worry about the rest of this list — your health comes first. If your injuries allow you to handle the remaining steps, do so, then proceed to the ER or urgent care as appropriate.

3. Make a report.

Contact law enforcement. New Mexico law requires reporting any motor vehicle accident involving bodily injury or apparent property damage of $500 or more — in practice, that's essentially every accident. If police are unable to respond to the scene, file a station report as soon as possible. Get the report number.

4. Get the other driver's insurance information.

Do not negotiate with the other driver. Politely ask for their insurance information and take a photo of their card if they're willing. If they refuse or become confrontational, let law enforcement handle it.

5. Preserve evidence.

Take photographs of the scene, the vehicles, and any visible injuries. Do this before the vehicles are moved if possible. The more documentation, the better.

APPENDIX C
QUESTIONS TO ASK BEFORE HIRING A LAWYER

Use these questions when meeting with an attorney to evaluate whether they're the right fit for your case. Pay attention not just to the answers, but to how they answer—patience, clarity, and respect matter as much as the substance.

About Their Practice

- Do you regularly handle car accident injury cases?
- Do you have experience with insurance coverage disputes, not just liability claims?
- What's your approach to investigating the insurance situation in a case like mine?
- Who will actually be working on my case? Will it be you or someone else at the firm?
- Are you licensed in New Mexico? Do you have experience in New Mexico courts?

About Fees and Costs

- What is your fee percentage?
- Are your fees different if we file a lawsuit? If we go to trial?

- How are case costs handled? Do you advance them, or will I need to pay as we go?
- Will I receive a cost breakdown before settling?
- If I already have a settlement offer, will your fee be calculated on the total settlement or just the increase you achieve?

About the Process

- How will we know when it's time to settle?
- How do you advise clients who are unsure whether a settlement offer is appropriate?
- Walk me through the claims negotiation process.
- Walk me through what litigation looks like if we have to sue.
- How will you investigate this case?

About Communication

- How often will I hear from you or your office?
- Who should I contact if I have questions?
- How quickly can I expect a response?

About My Specific Situation

- Based on what I've told you, what issues do you see in my case?
- Are there any concerns about liability or coverage?
- Do you see anything that might complicate my claim?

Red Flags to Watch For

Walk away if you encounter any of these:

- High-pressure tactics urging you to sign up immediately
- Confusing fee arrangements, especially fees that increase if certain events happen

- Guarantees or promises of specific results
- Dismissing or minimizing your legitimate questions
- Claims of special relationships with adjusters or judges
- Offers of money or gifts to sign with them
- They contacted you after the accident without you reaching out first

Yellow Flags to Consider

These aren't necessarily deal-breakers, but they may signal the fit isn't right:

- The attorney seemed rushed or inattentive
- Their explanations didn't make sense to you
- You felt like you were on different wavelengths
- They lacked confidence or clarity

After the Meeting, Ask Yourself

- Did I feel treated with respect?
- Did the attorney listen to my situation before jumping to conclusions?
- Will I be comfortable entrusting this person with a significant financial matter?
- Can I see myself working with this person for potentially years?

If you can answer yes to these questions, you may have found the right attorney. If you have doubts, keep looking.

APPENDIX D
QUESTIONS TO ASK YOUR LAWYER DURING YOUR CASE

Once you've hired an attorney, staying engaged means asking the right questions at the right times. Use these questions throughout your case to understand what's happening and participate in key decisions.

At the Start of Your Case

- What information do you need from me to get started?
- What should I do if the insurance company contacts me directly?
- How should I document my injuries and recovery?
- Is there anything I should avoid doing or saying while my case is pending?

About Insurance and Coverage

- What insurance policies might apply to my case?
- Have you looked into whether I have UM/UIM coverage that could apply?
- Are there any coverage issues we need to address?
- Has the at-fault driver's insurance company accepted liability?
- What are the policy limits we're dealing with?

During Medical Treatment

- Should I notify you when my treatment changes or when I see a new provider?
- How do I handle medical bills that arrive while my case is pending?
- Is there anything I need to know about my health insurance and subrogation?
- Do I have Medicare, Medicaid, or other coverage that requires special handling?
- What happens if I need treatment that my health insurance won't cover?

About Case Progress

- What stage is my case in right now?
- What are the next steps?
- Is there anything holding up progress on my case?
- What's your current timeline estimate?
- Is there anything you need from me?

When a Settlement Offer Comes In

- What is the offer?
- How does this compare to similar cases?
- Do you think this is a fair offer?
- What are the risks if we reject this and continue?
- What costs will we incur if we keep going?
- If we accept, what will my actual take-home amount be after fees, costs, and subrogation?

If Litigation Becomes Necessary

- Why do you recommend filing a lawsuit at this point?
- How will filing a lawsuit change the timeline and costs?

- What should I expect during discovery?
- How should I prepare for my deposition?
- What are the realistic outcomes if this goes to trial?

Before Settling

- Are all my medical bills and records accounted for?
- Have we identified and addressed all subrogation and lien claims?
- Do I have any Medicare issues that need to be resolved?
- What will the final disbursement look like?
- Is there anything I should consider before agreeing to settle?
- Once I sign, is this truly final—no possibility of coming back for more?

General Questions for Any Stage

- Is there anything about my case I should be concerned about?
- Is there anything I can do to help move things forward?
- When should I expect to hear from you next?
- What's the best way to reach you if I have questions?

Tips for Good Communication

- Keep a list of questions as they come up so you don't forget them.
- When you contact the office, be specific about what you need.
- Respond promptly when your attorney's office contacts you.
- Keep your attorney informed about changes—new address, new insurance, new medical providers, changes in your condition.
- If something doesn't make sense, ask for clarification. There are no stupid questions about your own case.

APPENDIX E
DOCUMENT CHECKLIST

Your attorney will need various documents to build your case. Use this checklist to gather and organize materials. Not every item will apply to every case—collect what's relevant to your situation.

About the Accident

- Police crash report
- Copy of your driver's license
- Photos of the accident scene
- Photos of vehicle damage
- Photos of your visible injuries
- Contact information for witnesses
- Written statements from witnesses
- Your own written account of what happened (as detailed as possible, as soon as possible after the accident)

Insurance Information

- Your auto insurance policy declarations page
- Your auto insurance policy (full document, if available)
- Declarations pages for other vehicles in your household
- Declarations pages for auto policies of other people who live with you

- The at-fault driver's insurance information (company, policy number, claim number)
- Your health insurance card and policy information
- Medicare card (if applicable)
- Medicaid card (if applicable)
- Any other insurance that might apply (umbrella policy, employer coverage, etc.)

Medical Treatment

- List of all medical providers you've seen for accident-related treatment (names, addresses, dates)
- Emergency room records
- Hospital admission and discharge records
- Primary care physician records
- Specialist records (orthopedic, neurology, pain management, etc.)
- Physical therapy records
- Chiropractic records
- Imaging results (X-rays, MRIs, CT scans)
- Prescription records
- Medical bills from all providers
- Explanation of Benefits (EOB) statements from your health insurer

Lost Wages and Employment

- Pay stubs from before the accident (to establish your normal earnings)
- Documentation of missed work dates
- Letter from employer confirming time missed and wages lost
- Tax returns (if self-employed or if income varies)
- Documentation of lost business opportunities (if self-employed)

Out-of-Pocket Expenses

- Receipts for medications
- Receipts for medical equipment (crutches, braces, etc.)
- Receipts for transportation to medical appointments
- Receipts for household help or childcare necessitated by your injuries
- Receipts for any other accident-related expenses

Property Damage

- Repair estimates for your vehicle
- Photos of vehicle damage (before repair)
- Pre-accident actual cash value (ACV) evaluation from insurance company
- Total loss packet (if your vehicle was totaled and the insurance company provided one)
- Gap insurance policy (if you have it)
- Rental car receipts
- Documentation of personal property damaged in the accident

Prior Medical History (if relevant)

- Records of any preexisting conditions that may have been aggravated
- Records from prior accidents or injuries to the same body parts

Legal and Court Documents (if litigation is filed)

- Any documents served on you related to the case
- Correspondence from the other party's attorney or insurance company
- Copies of anything you've signed related to the case or the accident

Communications to Save

- Letters or emails from insurance companies
- Notes from phone calls with adjusters (date, time, who you spoke with, what was discussed)
- Any recorded statements you've given (request copies if you don't have them)

Tips for Staying Organized

- Create a dedicated folder (physical or digital) for all accident-related documents.
- Date everything.
- Keep a running list of medical providers and appointment dates.
- Save originals and provide copies to your attorney.
- When in doubt about whether something is relevant, keep it and let your attorney decide.

505 Legal, P.C.

(505) 421-3329

www.505legal.com

www.ingramcontent.com/pod-product-compliance
Lightning Source LLC
Chambersburg PA
CBHW022102160426
43198CB00008B/320